GEORGE W. BUSH
Speaks to America

GEORGE W. BUSH
Speaks to America

Speeches Selected
By Alan Gottlieb

MERRIL PRESS
BELLEVUE, WASHINGTON

George W. Bush Speaks to the Nation is published by Merril
Press, P.O. Box 1682, Bellevue, WA 98009. Additional
copies of this book may be ordered from Merril Press at
$9.95 each. Phone: 425-454-7009. Book designed by
Tiffany Lindsay. Cover photo by AP World Wide photogra-
pher, Harry Cabluck.

FIRST EDITION

ISBN 0-936783-40-0

Library of Congress Cataloging-in-Publication Data

Bush, George W. (George Walker), 1946-
    George W. Bush speaks to the nation: speeches / selected
by Alan Gottlieb.-- 1st ed.
        p. cm.
    ISBN 0-936783-40-0
    1. Bush, George W. (George Walker), 1946- 2. Presi-
dents--United States--Messages. 3. United States--Politics
and government--2001- I. Gottlieb, Alan M. II. Title.

J82.E8 2004
352.23'8'0973--dc22   2004042605

PRINTED IN THE UNITED STATES OF AMERICA

DEDICATION

To my children Amy Jean, Sarah Merril, Alexis Hope, Andrew Michael, and all the other children of our nation. I hope they will continue to enjoy the freedom and liberty in their future that I have experienced thanks to the sacrifices made by the generations of Americans who came before us.

CONTENTS

FORWARD

This collection of important and inspiring speeches made by President George W. Bush clearly demonstrates the understanding that he has for our history and the challenges posed to our nation by the events of September 11, 2001.

Our country faces an enemy that President Bush described, like Churchill described the Nazis, as one that seeks to throw the world "into the abyss of a new Dark Age." Many of these included speeches are an expression of the determination and resolve to prevail over the forces of unspeakable horror and evil. It is a fight that we will win with President Bush's leadership. The included speeches are classics of American thought that will be read by future generations for many years to come.

If you haven't paid close attention to these vital speeches, then this book is a must read. Reading this collection of speeches, one can only praise the heartfelt passion of President Bush that is the cornerstone of his courageous leadership. As you read these speeches you will feel his desire to preserve our nation's freedom.

Yes, September 11th changed everything. It changed the Bush presidency. It allowed Americans to understand the reason why it was critical that George Bush was elected to the highest office in the land. He is a great leader in a time of crisis.

His State of the Union Address on January 28, 2003, proves his intelligence- which is, at best, ignored by the dominant media, or, at worst, ridiculed. However, no one can deny that every time he speaks to America, his poll numbers go up, not down, despite all the political pundits that try to convince the public that he isn't well-spoken.

Now paragraph by paragraph, sentence by sentence, word by word, you can judge for yourself.

Alan Gottlieb
Bellevue, Washington

Inaugural Address

Joint Session of Congress
January 20, 2001

President Clinton, distinguished guests and my fellow citizens, the peaceful transfer of authority is rare in history, yet common in our country. With a simple oath, we affirm old traditions and make new beginnings.

As I begin, I thank President Clinton for his service to our nation.

And I thank Vice President Gore for a contest conducted with spirit and ended with grace.

I am honored and humbled to stand here, where so many of America's leaders have come before me, and so many will follow.

We have a place, all of us, in a long story—a story we continue, but whose end we will not see. It is the story of a new world that became a friend and liberator of the old, a story of a slave-holding society that became a servant of freedom, the story of a power that went into the world to protect but not possess, to defend but not to conquer.

It is the American story—a story of flawed and fallible people, united across the generations by grand and enduring ideals.

The grandest of these ideals is an unfolding American promise that everyone belongs, that everyone deserves a chance, that no insignificant person was ever born.

Americans are called to enact this promise in our lives and in our laws. And though our nation has sometimes halted, and sometimes delayed, we must follow no other course.

Through much of the last century, America's faith in freedom and democracy was a rock in a raging sea. Now it is a seed upon the wind, taking root in many nations.

Our democratic faith is more than the creed of our country, it is the inborn hope of our humanity, an ideal we carry but do not own, a trust we bear and pass along. And even after nearly 225 years, we have a long way yet to travel.

While many of our citizens prosper, others doubt the promise, even the justice, of our own country. The ambitions of some Americans are limited by failing schools and hidden prejudice and the circumstances of their birth. And sometimes our differences run so deep, it seems we share a continent, but not a country.

We do not accept this, and we will not allow it. Our unity, our union, is the serious work of leaders and citizens in every generation. And this is my solemn pledge: I will work to build a single nation of justice and opportunity.

I know this is in our reach because we are guided by a power larger than ourselves who creates us equal in His image.

And we are confident in principles that unite and lead us onward.

America has never been united by blood or birth or soil. We are bound by ideals that move us beyond our backgrounds, lift us above our interests and teach us what it means to be citizens. Every child must be taught these principles. Every citizen must uphold them. And every immigrant, by embracing these ideals, makes our country more, not less, American.

Today, we affirm a new commitment to live out our nation's promise through civility, courage, compassion and character.

America, at its best, matches a commitment to principle with a concern for civility. A civil society demands from each of us good will and respect, fair dealing and forgiveness.

Some seem to believe that our politics can afford to be

petty because, in a time of peace, the stakes of our debates appear small.

But the stakes for America are never small. If our country does not lead the cause of freedom, it will not be led. If we do not turn the hearts of children toward knowledge and character, we will lose their gifts and undermine their idealism. If we permit our economy to drift and decline, the vulnerable will suffer most.

We must live up to the calling we share. Civility is not a tactic or a sentiment. It is the determined choice of trust over cynicism, of community over chaos. And this commitment, if we keep it, is a way to shared accomplishment.

America, at its best, is also courageous.

Our national courage has been clear in times of depression and war, when defending common dangers defined our common good. Now we must choose if the example of our fathers and mothers will inspire us or condemn us. We must show courage in a time of blessing by confronting problems instead of passing them on to future generations.

Together, we will reclaim America's schools, before ignorance and apathy claim more young lives.

We will reform Social Security and Medicare, sparing our children from struggles we have the power to prevent. And we will reduce taxes, to recover the momentum of our economy and reward the effort and enterprise of working Americans.

We will build our defenses beyond challenge, lest weakness invite challenge.

We will confront weapons of mass destruction, so that a new century is spared new horrors.

The enemies of liberty and our country should make no mistake: America remains engaged in the world by history and by choice, shaping a balance of power that favors freedom. We will defend our allies and our interests. We will show purpose without arrogance. We will meet aggression and bad faith with resolve and strength. And to all nations, we will speak for the values that gave our nation birth.

America, at its best, is compassionate. In the quiet of American conscience, we know that deep, persistent poverty is unworthy of our nation's promise.

And whatever our views of its cause, we can agree that children at risk are not at fault. Abandonment and abuse are not acts of God, they are failures of love.

And the proliferation of prisons, however necessary, is no substitute for hope and order in our souls.

Where there is suffering, there is duty. Americans in need are not strangers, they are citizens, not problems, but priorities. And all of us are diminished when any are hopeless.

Government has great responsibilities for public safety and public health, for civil rights and common schools. Yet compassion is the work of a nation, not just a government.

And some needs and hurts are so deep they will only respond to a mentor's touch or a pastor's prayer. Church and charity, synagogue and mosque lend our communities their humanity, and they will have an honored place in our plans and in our laws.

Many in our country do not know the pain of poverty, but we can listen to those who do.

And I can pledge our nation to a goal: When we see that wounded traveler on the road to Jericho, we will not pass to the other side.

America, at its best, is a place where personal responsibility is valued and expected.

Encouraging responsibility is not a search for scapegoats, it is a call to conscience. And though it requires sacrifice, it brings a deeper fulfillment. We find the fullness of life not only in options, but in commitments. And we find that children and community are the commitments that set us free.

Our public interest depends on private character, on

civic duty and family bonds and basic fairness, on uncounted, unhonored acts of decency which give direction to our freedom.

Sometimes in life we are called to do great things. But as a saint of our times has said, every day we are called to do small things with great love. The most important tasks of a democracy are done by everyone.

I will live and lead by these principles: to advance my convictions with civility, to pursue the public interest with courage, to speak for greater justice and compassion, to call for responsibility and try to live it as well.

In all these ways, I will bring the values of our history to the care of our times.

What you do is as important as anything government does. I ask you to seek a common good beyond your comfort; to defend needed reforms against easy attacks; to serve your nation, beginning with your neighbor. I ask you to be citizens: citizens, not spectators; citizens, not subjects; responsible citizens, building communities of service and a nation of character.

Americans are generous and strong and decent, not because we believe in ourselves, but because we hold beliefs beyond ourselves. When this spirit of citizenship is missing, no government program can replace it. When this spirit is present, no wrong can stand against it.

After the Declaration of Independence was signed, Virginia statesman John Page wrote to Thomas Jefferson: "We know the race is not to the swift nor the battle to the strong. Do you not think an angel rides in the whirlwind and directs this storm?"

Much time has passed since Jefferson arrived for his inauguration. The years and changes accumulate. But the themes of this day he would know: our nation's grand story of courage and its simple dream of dignity.

We are not this story's author, who fills time and eternity with his purpose. Yet his purpose is achieved in our duty, and our duty is fulfilled in service to one another.

Never tiring, never yielding, never finishing, we renew that purpose today, to make our country more just and generous, to affirm the dignity of our lives and every life.

This work continues. This story goes on. And an angel still rides in the whirlwind and directs this storm.

God bless you all, and God bless America.

NATIONAL DAY OF PRAYER AND REMEMBRANCE

We are here in the middle hour of our grief. So many have suffered so great a loss, and today we express our nation's sorrow. We come before God to pray for the missing and the dead, and for those who love them.

On Tuesday, our country was attacked with deliberate and massive cruelty. We have seen the images of fire and ashes, and bent steel.

Now come the names, the list of casualties we are only beginning to read. They are the names of men and women who began their day at a desk or in an airport, busy with life. They are the names of people who faced death, and in their last moments called home to say, be brave, and I love you.

They are the names of passengers who defied their murderers, and prevented the murder of others on the ground. They are the names of men and women who wore the uniform of the United States, and died at their posts.

They are the names of rescuers, the ones whom death found running up the stairs and into the fires to help others. We will read all these names. We will linger over them, and learn their stories, and many Americans will weep.

To the children and parents and spouses and families and friends of the lost, we offer the deepest sympathy of the nation. And I assure you, you are not alone.

Just three days removed from these events, Americans do not yet have the distance of history. But our responsibility to history is already clear: to answer these attacks and rid the world of evil.

War has been waged against us by stealth and deceit and

murder. This nation is peaceful, but fierce when stirred to anger. This conflict was begun on the timing and terms of others. It will end in a way, and at an hour, of our choosing.

Our purpose as a nation is firm. Yet our wounds as a people are recent and unhealed, and lead us to pray. In many of our prayers this week, there is a searching, and an honesty. At St. Patrick's Cathedral in New York on Tuesday, a woman said, "I prayed to God to give us a sign that He is still here." Others have prayed for the same, searching hospital to hospital, carrying pictures of those still missing.

God's signs are not always the ones we look for. We learn in tragedy that his purposes are not always our own. Yet the prayers of private suffering, whether in our homes or in this great cathedral, are known and heard, and understood.

There are prayers that help us last through the day, or endure the night. There are prayers of friends and strangers, that give us strength for the journey. And there are prayers that yield our will to a will greater than our own.

This world He created is of moral design. Grief and tragedy and hatred are only for a time. Goodness, remembrance, and love have no end. And the Lord of life holds all who die, and all who mourn.

It is said that adversity introduces us to ourselves. This is true of a nation as well. In this trial, we have been reminded, and the world has seen, that our fellow Americans are generous and kind, resourceful and brave. We see our national character in rescuers working past exhaustion; in long lines of blood donors; in thousands of citizens who have asked to work and serve in any way possible.

And we have seen our national character in eloquent acts of sacrifice. Inside the World Trade Center, one man who could have saved himself stayed until the end at the side of his quadriplegic friend. A beloved priest died giving the last rites to a firefighter. Two office workers, finding a disabled stranger, carried her down sixty-eight floors to safety. A group of men drove through the night from Dallas to Washington to bring skin grafts for burn victims.

In these acts, and in many others, Americans showed a deep commitment to one another, and an abiding love for our country. Today, we feel what Franklin Roosevelt called the warm courage of national unity. This is a unity of every faith, and every background.

It has joined together political parties in both houses of Congress. It is evident in services of prayer and candlelight vigils, and American flags, which are displayed in pride, and wave in defiance.

Our unity is a kinship of grief, and a steadfast resolve to prevail against our enemies. And this unity against terror is now extending across the world.

America is a nation full of good fortune, with so much to be grateful for. But we are not spared from suffering. In every generation, the world has produced enemies of human freedom. They have attacked America, because we are freedom's home and defender. And the commitment of our fathers is now the calling of our time.

On this national day of prayer and remembrance, we ask almighty God to watch over our nation, and grant us patience and resolve in all that is to come. We pray that He will comfort and console those who now walk in sorrow. We thank Him for each life we now must mourn, and the promise of a life to come.

As we have been assured, neither death nor life, nor angels nor principalities nor powers, nor things present nor things to come, nor height nor depth, can separate us from God's love. May He bless the souls of the departed. May He comfort our own. And may He always guide our country.

God bless America.

DECLARATION OF WAR ON TERROR

JOINT SESSION OF CONGRESS
SEPTEMBER 20, 2001

In the normal course of events, Presidents come to this chamber to report on the state of the Union. Tonight, no such report is needed. It has already been delivered by the American people.

We have seen it in the courage of passengers, who rushed terrorists to save others on the ground — passengers like an exceptional man named Todd Beamer. Please help me to welcome his wife, Lisa Beamer, here tonight.

We have seen the state of our Union in the endurance of rescuers, working past exhaustion. We have seen the unfurling of flags, the lighting of candles, the giving of blood, the saying of prayers — in English, Hebrew, and Arabic. We have seen the decency of a loving and giving people, who have made the grief of strangers their own.

My fellow citizens, for the last nine days, the entire world has seen for itself the state of our Union — and it is strong.

Tonight we are a country awakened to danger and called to defend freedom. Our grief has turned to anger, and anger to resolution. Whether we bring our enemies to justice, or bring justice to our enemies, justice will be done.

I thank the Congress for its leadership at such an important time. All of America was touched on the evening of the tragedy to see Republicans and Democrats, joined together on the steps of this Capitol, singing "God Bless America." And you did more than sing, you acted, by delivering forty billion dollars to rebuild our communities and meet the needs of our military.

Speaker Hastert and Minority Leader Gephardt — Majority Leader Daschle and Senator Lott — I thank you for your friendship and your leadership and your service to our country.

And on behalf of the American people, I thank the world for its outpouring of support. America will never forget the sounds of our National Anthem playing at Buckingham Palace, and on the streets of Paris, and at Berlin's Brandenburg Gate. We will not forget South Korean children gathering to pray outside our embassy in Seoul, or the prayers of sympathy offered at a mosque in Cairo. We will not forget moments of silence and days of mourning in Australia and Africa and Latin America.

Nor will we forget the citizens of eighty other nations who died with our own. Dozens of Pakistanis. More than 130 Israelis. More than 250 citizens of India. Men and women from El Salvador, Iran, Mexico, and Japan. And hundreds of British citizens. America has no truer friend than Great Britain. Once again, we are joined together in a great cause. The British Prime Minister has crossed an ocean to show his unity of purpose with America, and tonight we welcome Tony Blair.

On September the eleventh, enemies of freedom committed an act of war against our country. Americans have known wars — but for the past 136 years, they have been wars on foreign soil, except for one Sunday in 1941. Americans have known the casualties of war — but not at the center of a great city on a peaceful morning. Americans have known surprise attacks — but never before on thousands of civilians. All of this was brought upon us in a single day — and night fell on a different world, a world where freedom itself is under attack.

Americans have many questions tonight. Americans are asking: Who attacked our country?

The evidence we have gathered all points to a collection of loosely affiliated terrorist organizations known as al-Qaida. They are the same murderers indicted for bombing American embassies in Tanzania and Kenya, and responsible for the bombing of the U.S.S. Cole.

Al-Qaida is to terror what the Mafia is to crime. But its goal is not making money; its goal is remaking the world — and imposing its radical beliefs on people everywhere.

The terrorists practice a fringe form of Islamic extremism that has been rejected by Muslim scholars and the vast majority of Muslim clerics — a fringe movement that perverts the peaceful teachings of Islam. The terrorists? directive commands them to kill Christians and Jews, to kill all Americans, and make no distinctions among military and civilians, including women and children.

This group and its leader — a person named Osama bin Ladin — are linked to many other organizations in different countries, including the Egyptian Islamic Jihad and the Islamic Movement of Uzbekistan.

There are thousands of these terrorists in more than sixty countries. They are recruited from their own nations and neighborhoods, and brought to camps in places like Afghanistan where they are trained in the tactics of terror. They are sent back to their homes or sent to hide in countries around the world to plot evil and destruction.

The leadership of al-Qaida has great influence in Afghanistan, and supports the Taliban regime in controlling most of that country. In Afghanistan, we see al-Qaida's vision for the world.

Afghanistan's people have been brutalized — many are starving and many have fled. Women are not allowed to attend school. You can be jailed for owning a television. Religion can be practiced only as their leaders dictate. A man can be jailed in Afghanistan if his beard is not long enough.

The United States respects the people of Afghanistan — after all, we are currently its largest source of humanitarian aid — but we condemn the Taliban regime. It is not only repressing its own people, it is threatening people everywhere by sponsoring and sheltering and supplying terrorists. By aiding and abetting murder, the Taliban regime is committing murder. And tonight, the United States of America makes the following demands on the Taliban:

Deliver to United States authorities all the leaders of al-Qaida who hide in your land.

Release all foreign nationals — including American citizens — you have unjustly imprisoned, and protect foreign journalists, diplomats, and aid workers in your country.

Close immediately and permanently every terrorist training camp in Afghanistan and hand over every terrorist, and every person in their support structure, to appropriate authorities.

Give the United States full access to terrorist training camps, so we can make sure they are no longer operating.

These demands are not open to negotiation or discussion. The Taliban must act and act immediately. They will hand over the terrorists, or they will share in their fate.

I also want to speak tonight directly to Muslims throughout the world: We respect your faith. It is practiced freely by many millions of Americans, and by millions more in countries that America counts as friends. Its teachings are good and peaceful, and those who commit evil in the name of Allah blaspheme the name of Allah. The terrorists are traitors to their own faith, trying, in effect, to hijack Islam itself. The enemy of America is not our many Muslim friends; it is not our many Arab friends. Our enemy is a radical network of terrorists, and every government that supports them.

Our war on terror begins with al-Qaida, but it does not end there. It will not end until every terrorist group of global reach has been found, stopped, and defeated.

Americans are asking: Why do they hate us?

They hate what we see right here in this chamber — a democratically elected government. Their leaders are self-appointed. They hate our freedoms — our freedom of religion, our freedom of speech, our freedom to vote and assemble and disagree with each other.

They want to overthrow existing governments in many Muslim countries, such as Egypt, Saudi Arabia, and Jordan. They want to drive Israel out of the Middle East. They want to drive Christians and Jews out of vast regions of Asia and Africa.

These terrorists kill not merely to end lives, but to disrupt and end a way of life. With every atrocity, they hope that America grows fearful, retreating from the world and forsaking our friends. They stand against us, because we stand in their way.

We are not deceived by their pretenses to piety. We have seen their kind before. They are the heirs of all the murderous ideologies of the twentieth century. By sacrificing human life to serve their radical visions — by abandoning every value except the will to power — they follow in the path of fascism, and Nazism, and totalitarianism. And they will follow that path all the way, to where it ends: in history's unmarked grave of discarded lies.

Americans are asking: How will we fight and win this war?

We will direct every resource at our command — every means of diplomacy, every tool of intelligence, every instrument of law enforcement, every financial influence, and every necessary weapon of war — to the disruption and defeat of the global terror network.

This war will not be like the war against Iraq a decade ago, with its decisive liberation of territory and its swift conclusion. It will not look like the air war above Kosovo two years ago, where no ground troops were used and not a single American was lost in combat.

Our response involves far more than instant retaliation and isolated strikes. Americans should not expect one battle, but a lengthy campaign, unlike any other we have seen. It may include dramatic strikes, visible on television, and covert operations, secret even in success. We will starve terrorists of funding, turn them one against another, drive them from place to place, until there is no refuge or rest. And we will pursue nations that provide aid or safe haven to terrorism. Every nation, in every region, now has a decision to make. Either you are with us, or you are with the terrorists. From this day forward, any nation that continues to harbor or support terrorism will be regarded by the United States as a hostile regime.

Our Nation has been put on notice: We are not immune from attack. We will take defensive measures against terrorism to protect Americans.

Today, dozens of federal departments and agencies, as well as state and local governments, have responsibilities affecting homeland security. These efforts must be coordinated at the highest level. So tonight I announce the creation of a Cabinet-level position reporting directly to me — the Office of Homeland Security.

These measures are essential. But the only way to defeat terrorism as a threat to our way of life is to stop it, eliminate it, and destroy it where it grows.

Many will be involved in this effort, from FBI agents to intelligence operatives to the reservists we have called to active duty. All deserve our thanks, and all have our prayers. And tonight, a few miles from the damaged Pentagon, I have a message for our military: Be ready. I have called the armed forces to alert, and there is a reason. The hour is coming when America will act, and you will make us proud.

This is not, however, just America's fight. And what is at stake is not just America's freedom. This is the world's fight. This is civilization's fight. This is the fight of all who believe in progress and pluralism, tolerance and freedom.

We ask every nation to join us. We will ask, and we will need, the help of police forces, intelligence services, and banking systems around the world. The United States is grateful that many nations and many international organizations have already responded — with sympathy and with support. Nations from Latin America, to Asia, to Africa, to Europe, to the Islamic world. Perhaps the NATO Charter reflects best the attitude of the world: an attack on one is an attack on all.

The civilized world is rallying to America's side. They understand that if this terror goes unpunished, their own cities, their own citizens may be next. Terror, unanswered, can not only bring down buildings, it can threaten the stability of legitimate governments. And we will not allow it.

Americans are asking: What is expected of us?

I ask you to live your lives and hug your children. I know many citizens have fears tonight, and I ask you to be calm and resolute, even in the face of a continuing threat.

I ask you to uphold the values of America, and remember why so many have come here. We are in a fight for our principles, and our first responsibility is to live by them. No one should be singled out for unfair treatment or unkind words because of their ethnic background or religious faith.

I ask you to continue to support the victims of this tragedy with your contributions. Those who want to give can go to a central source of information, libertyunites.org, to find the names of groups providing direct help in New York, Pennsylvania, and Virginia.

The thousands of FBI agents who are now at work in this investigation may need your cooperation, and I ask you to give it.

I ask for your patience, with the delays and inconveniences that may accompany tighter security — and for your patience in what will be a long struggle.

I ask your continued participation and confidence in the American economy. Terrorists attacked a symbol of American prosperity. They did not touch its source. America is successful because of the hard work, and creativity, and enterprise of our people. These were the true strengths of our economy before September eleventh, and they are our strengths today.

Finally, please continue praying for the victims of terror and their families, for those in uniform, and for our great country. Prayer has comforted us in sorrow, and will help strengthen us for the journey ahead.

Tonight I thank my fellow Americans for what you have already done and for what you will do. And ladies and gentlemen of the Congress, I thank you, their representatives, for what you have already done, and for what we will do together.

Tonight, we face new and sudden national challenges. We will come together to improve air safety, to dramatically expand the number of air marshals on domestic flights, and take new measures to prevent hijacking. We will come together to promote stability and keep our airlines flying with direct assistance during this emergency.

We will come together to give law enforcement the additional tools it needs to track down terror here at home. We will come together to strengthen our intelligence capabilities to know the plans of terrorists before they act, and find them before they strike.

We will come together to take active steps that strengthen America's economy, and put our people back to work.

Tonight we welcome here two leaders who embody the extraordinary spirit of all New Yorkers: Governor George Pataki, and Mayor Rudy Giuliani. As a symbol of America's resolve, my Administration will work with the Congress, and these two leaders, to show the world that we will rebuild New York City.

After all that has just passed — all the lives taken, and all the possibilities and hopes that died with them— it is natural to wonder if America's future is one of fear. Some speak of an age of terror. I know there are struggles ahead, and dangers to face. But this country will define our times, not be defined by them. As long as the United States of America is determined and strong, this will not be an age of terror; this will be an age of liberty, here and across the world.

Great harm has been done to us. We have suffered great loss. And in our grief and anger we have found our mission and our moment. Freedom and fear are at war. The advance of human freedom — the great achievement of our time, and the great hope of every time — now depends on us. Our Nation — this generation — will lift a dark threat of violence from our people and our future. We will rally the world to this cause, by our efforts and by our courage. We will not tire, we will not falter, and we will not fail.

It is my hope that in the months and years ahead, life will return almost to normal. We'll go back to our lives and routines, and that is good. Even grief recedes with time and grace. But our resolve must not pass. Each of us will remember what happened that day, and to whom it happened. We will remember the moment the news came — where we were and what we were doing. Some will remember an image of fire, or a story of rescue. Some will carry memories of a face and a voice gone forever.

And I will carry this. It is the police shield of a man named George Howard, who died at the World Trade Center trying to save others. It was given to me by his mom, Arlene, as a proud memorial to her son. This is my reminder of lives that ended, and a task that does not end.

I will not forget this wound to our country, or those who inflicted it. I will not yield — I will not rest — I will not relent in waging this struggle for the freedom and security of the American people.

The course of this conflict is not known, yet its outcome is certain. Freedom and fear, justice and cruelty, have always been at war, and we know that God is not neutral between them.

Fellow citizens, we will meet violence with patient justice — assured of the rightness of our cause, and confident of the victories to come. In all that lies before us, may God grant us wisdom, and may He watch over the United States of America.

2002 State of the Union

Joint Session of Congress
January 29, 2002

Mr. Speaker, Vice President Cheney, members of Congress, distinguished guests, fellow citizens, as we gather tonight, our nation is at war, our economy is in recession and the civilized world faces unprecedented dangers. Yet the state of our union has never been stronger.

We last met in an hour of shock and suffering. In four short months, our nation has comforted the victims, begun to rebuild New York and the Pentagon, rallied a great coalition, captured, arrested and rid the world of thousands of terrorists, destroyed Afghanistan's terrorist training camps, saved a people from starvation and freed a country from brutal oppression.

The American flag flies again over our embassy in Kabul. Terrorists who once occupied Afghanistan now occupy cells at Guantanamo Bay.

And terrorist leaders who urged followers to sacrifice their lives are running for their own.

America and Afghanistan are now allies against terror. We will be partners in rebuilding that country. And this evening we welcomed the distinguished interim leader of a liberated Afghanistan: Chairman Hamid Karzai.

The last time we met in this chamber, the mothers and daughters of Afghanistan were captives in their own homes, forbidden from working or going to school.

Today women are free, and are part of Afghanistan's new government. And we welcome the new minister of women's affairs, Dr. Sima Samar.

Our progress is a tribute to the spirit of the Afghan

people, to the resolve of our coalition and to the might of the United States military.

When I called our troops into action, I did so with complete confidence in their courage and skill. And tonight, thanks to them, we are winning the war on terror.

The men and women of our armed forces have delivered a message now clear to every enemy of the United States: Even 7,000 miles away, across oceans and continents, on mountain tops and in caves you will not escape the justice of this nation.

For many Americans, these four months have brought sorrow and pain that will never completely go away. Every day a retired firefighter returns to ground zero to feel closer to his two sons who died there.

At a memorial in New York, a little boy left his football with a note for his lost father: "Dear Daddy, please take this to Heaven. I don't want to play football until I can play with you again someday."

Last month, at the grave of her husband, Michael, a CIA officer and Marine who died in Mazar-i-Sharif, Shannon Spann said these words of farewell: "Semper fi, my love." Shannon is with us tonight.

Shannon, I assure you and all who have lost a loved one that our cause is just, and our country will never forget the debt we owe Michael and all who gave their lives for freedom.

Our cause is just, and it continues. Our discoveries in Afghanistan confirmed our worst fears and showed us the true scope of the task ahead. We have seen the depth of our enemies' hatred in videos where they laugh about the loss of innocent life.

And the depth of their hatred is equaled by the madness of the destruction they design. We have found diagrams of American nuclear power plants and public water facilities, detailed instructions for making chemical weapons, surveillance maps of American cities, and thorough descriptions of landmarks in America and throughout the world.

What we have found in Afghanistan confirms that, far from ending there, our war against terror is only beginning. Most of the 19 men who hijacked planes on September the 11th were trained in Afghanistan's camps. And so were tens of thousands of others. Thousands of dangerous killers, schooled in the methods of murder, often supported by outlaw regimes, are now spread throughout the world like ticking time bombs, set to go off without warning.

Thanks to the work of our law enforcement officials and coalition partners, hundreds of terrorists have been arrested, yet tens of thousands of trained terrorists are still at large. These enemies view the entire world as a battlefield, and we must pursue them wherever they are.

So long as training camps operate, so long as nations harbor terrorists, freedom is at risk and America and our allies must not, and will not, allow it. Our nation will continue to be steadfast, and patient and persistent in the pursuit of two great objectives. First, we will shut down terrorist camps, disrupt terrorist plans and bring terrorists to justice.

And second, we must prevent the terrorists and regimes who seek chemical, biological or nuclear weapons from threatening the United States and the world.

Our military has put the terror training camps of Afghanistan out of business, yet camps still exist in at least a dozen countries. A terrorist underworld — including groups like Hamas, Hezbollah, Islamic Jihad and Jaish-i-Mohammed — operates in remote jungles and deserts, and hides in the centers of large cities.

While the most visible military action is in Afghanistan, America is acting elsewhere.

We now have troops in the Philippines helping to train that country's armed forces to go after terrorist cells that have executed an American and still hold hostages.

Our soldiers, working with the Bosnian government, seized terrorists who were plotting to bomb our embassy.

Our Navy is patrolling the coast of Africa to block the shipment of weapons and the establishment of terrorist camps in Somalia.

My hope is that all nations will heed our call and eliminate the terrorist parasites who threaten their countries and our own.

Many nations are acting forcefully. Pakistan is now cracking down on terror, and I admire the strong leadership of President Musharraf.

But some governments will be timid in the face of terror. And make no mistake about it: If they do not act, America will.

Our second goal is to prevent regimes that sponsor terror from threatening America or our friends and allies with weapons of mass destruction.

Some of these regimes have been pretty quiet since September 11, but we know their true nature. North Korea is a regime arming with missiles and weapons of mass destruction, while starving its citizens.

Iran aggressively pursues these weapons and exports terror, while an un-elected few repress the Iranian people's hope for freedom.

Iraq continues to flaunt its hostility toward America and to support terror. The Iraqi regime has plotted to develop anthrax and nerve gas and nuclear weapons for over a decade.

This is a regime that has already used poison gas to murder thousands of its own citizens, leaving the bodies of mothers huddled over their dead children. This is a regime that agreed to international inspections then kicked out the inspectors. This is a regime that has something to hide from the civilized world.

States like these, and their terrorist allies, constitute an axis of evil, arming to threaten the peace of the world. By seeking weapons of mass destruction, these regimes pose a grave and growing danger. They could provide these arms to terrorists, giving them the means to match their hatred. They could attack our allies or attempt to blackmail the United States. In any of these cases, the price of indifference would be catastrophic.

We will work closely with our coalition to deny terrorists and their state sponsors the materials, technology and expertise to make and deliver weapons of mass destruction.

We will develop and deploy effective missile defenses to protect America and our allies from sudden attack.

And all nations should know: America will do what is necessary to ensure our nation's security.

We'll be deliberate, yet time is not on our side. I will not wait on events while dangers gather. I will not stand by as peril draws closer and closer. The United States of America will not permit the world's most dangerous regimes to threaten us with the world's most destructive weapons.

Our war on terror is well begun, but it is only begun. This campaign may not be finished on our watch, yet it must be and it will be waged on our watch.

We can't stop short. If we stopped now, leaving terror camps intact and terror states unchecked, our sense of security would be false and temporary. History has called America and our allies to action, and it is both our responsibility and our privilege to fight freedom's fight.

Our first priority must always be the security of our nation, and that will be reflected in the budget I send to Congress. My budget supports three great goals for America: We will win this war, we will protect our homeland, and we will revive our economy.

September 11 brought out the best in America and the best in this Congress, and I join the American people in applauding your unity and resolve.

Now Americans deserve to have this same spirit directed toward addressing problems here at home.

I am a proud member of my party. Yet as we act to win the war, protect our people and create jobs in America, we must act first and foremost not as Republicans, not as Democrats, but as Americans.

It costs a lot to fight this war. We have spent more than a billion dollars a month — over $30 million a day — and we must be prepared for future operations. Afghanistan proved that expensive precision weapons defeat the enemy and spare innocent lives, and we need more of them. We need to replace aging aircraft and make our military more agile to put our troops anywhere in the world quickly and safely.

Our men and women in uniform deserve the best weapons, the best equipment and the best training and they also deserve another pay raise.

My budget includes the largest increase in defense spending in two decades, because while the price of freedom and security is high, it is never too high. Whatever it costs to defend our country, we will pay.

The next priority of my budget is to do everything possible to protect our citizens and strengthen our nation against the ongoing threat of another attack.

Time and distance from the events of September the 11th will not make us safer unless we act on its lessons. America is no longer protected by vast oceans. We are protected from attack only by vigorous action abroad and increased vigilance at home.

My budget nearly doubles funding for a sustained strategy of homeland security, focused on four key areas: bioterrorism, emergency response, airport and border security, and improved intelligence.

We will develop vaccines to fight anthrax and other deadly diseases. We'll increase funding to help states and communities train and equip our heroic police and firefighters.

We will improve intelligence collection and sharing, expand patrols at our borders, strengthen the security of air travel, and use technology to track the arrivals and departures of visitors to the United States.

Homeland security will make America not only stronger but in many ways better. Knowledge gained from bioterrorism research will improve public health. Stronger police and fire departments will mean safer neighborhoods. Stricter border enforcement will help combat illegal drugs.

And as government works to better secure our homeland, America will continue to depend on the eyes and ears of alert citizens.

A few days before Christmas, an airline flight attendant spotted a passenger lighting a match. The crew and passengers quickly subdued the man, who had been trained by Al Qaeda and was armed with explosives. The people on that airplane were alert, and as a result likely saved nearly 200 lives. And tonight we welcome and thank flight attendants Hermis Moutardier and Christina Jones.

Once we have funded our national security and our homeland security, the final great priority of my budget is economic security for the American people.

To achieve these great national objectives — to win the war, protect the homeland and revitalize our economy — our budget will run a deficit that will be small and short term so long as Congress restrains spending and acts in a fiscally responsible way.

We have clear priorities and we must act at home with the same purpose and resolve we have shown overseas. We will prevail in the war, and we will defeat this recession.

Americans who have lost their jobs need our help, and I support extending unemployment benefits and direct assistance for health care coverage.

Yet American workers want more than unemployment checks. They want a steady paycheck.

When America works, America prospers, so my economic security plan can be summed up in one word: jobs.

Good jobs begin with good schools, and here we've made a fine start.

Republicans and Democrats worked together to achieve historic education reform so that no child is left behind.

I was proud to work with members of both parties, Chairman John Boehner and Congressman George Miller and Senator Judd Gregg.

And I was so proud of our work I even had nice things to say about my friend Ted Kennedy.

I know the folks at the Crawford coffee shop couldn't believe I'd say such a thing. But our work on this bill shows what is possible if we set aside posturing and focus on results.

There's more to do. We need to prepare our children to read and succeed in school with improved Head Start and early childhood development programs.

We must upgrade our teacher colleges and teacher training and launch a major recruiting drive with a great goal for America: a quality teacher in every classroom.

Good jobs also depend on reliable and affordable energy. This Congress must act to encourage conservation, promote technology, build infrastructure, and it must act to increase energy production at home so America is less dependent on foreign oil.

Good jobs depend on expanded trade. Selling into new markets creates new jobs, so I ask Congress to finally approve trade promotion authority.

On these two key issues, trade and energy, the House of Representatives has acted to create jobs and I urge the Senate to pass this legislation.

Good jobs depend on sound tax policy. Last year, some in this hall thought my tax relief plan was too small, some thought it was too big.

But when those checks arrived in the mail, most Americans thought tax relief was just about right.

Congress listened to the people and responded by reducing tax rates, doubling the child credit and ending the death tax. For the sake of long-term growth, and to help Americans plan for the future, let's make these tax cuts permanent.

The way out of this recession, the way to create jobs, is to grow the economy by encouraging investment in factories and equipment, and by speeding up tax relief so people have more money to spend.

For the sake of American workers, let's pass a stimulus package.

Good jobs must be the aim of welfare reform. As we reauthorize these important reforms, we must always remember: The goal is to reduce dependency on government and offer every American the dignity of a job.

Americans know economic security can vanish in an instant without health security. I ask Congress to join me this year to enact a patients' bill of rights to give uninsured workers credits to help buy health coverage to approve an historic increase in spending for veterans' health and to give seniors a sound and modern Medicare system that includes coverage for prescription drugs.

A good jobs — a good job should lead to security in retirement. I ask Congress to enact new safeguards for 401(k) and pension plans.

Employees who have worked hard and saved all their lives should not have to risk losing everything if their company fails.

Through stricter accounting standards and tougher disclosure requirements, corporate America must be made more accountable to employees and shareholders and held to the highest standards of conduct.

Retirement security also depends upon keeping the

commitments of Social Security, and we will. We must make Social Security financially stable and allow personal retirement accounts for younger workers who choose them.

Members, you and I will work together in the months ahead on other issues: productive farm policy a cleaner environment broader home ownership, especially among minorities and ways to encourage the good work of charities and faith- based groups.

I ask you to join me on these important domestic issues in the same spirit of cooperation we have applied to our war against terrorism.

During these last few months, I've been humbled and privileged to see the true character of this country in a time of testing. Our enemies believed America was weak and materialistic, that we would splinter in fear and selfishness. They were as wrong as they are evil.

The American people have responded magnificently, with courage and compassion, strength and resolve. As I have met the heroes, hugged the families and looked into the tired faces of rescuers, I have stood in awe of the American people.

And I hope you will join me in expressing thanks to one American for the strength and calm and comfort she brings to our nation in crisis: our first lady, Laura Bush.

None of us would ever wish the evil that was done on September the 11th, yet after America was attacked, it was as if our entire country looked into a mirror and saw our better selves. We were reminded that we are citizens with obligations to each other, to our country, and to history. We began to think less of the goods we can accumulate, and more about the good we can do.

For too long our culture has said, "If it feels good, do it." Now America is embracing a new ethic and a new creed: "Let's roll."

In the sacrifice of soldiers, the fierce brotherhood of firefighters, and the bravery and generosity of ordinary citizens, we have glimpsed what a new culture of responsibility could look like. We want to be a nation that serves goals larger than self. We have been offered a unique opportunity, and we must not let this moment pass.

My call tonight is for every American to commit at least two years — 4,000 hours — over the rest of your lifetime to the service of your neighbors and your nation.

Many are already serving, and I thank you. If you aren't sure how to help, I've got a good place to start. To sustain and extend the best that has emerged in America, I invite you to join the new USA Freedom Corps. The Freedom Corps will focus on three areas of need: responding in case of crisis at home, rebuilding our communities, and extending American compassion throughout the world.

One purpose of the USA Freedom Corps will be homeland security. America needs retired doctors and nurses who can be mobilized in major emergencies, volunteers to help police and fire departments, transportation and utility workers well trained in spotting danger.

Our country also needs citizens working to rebuild our communities. We need mentors to love children, especially children whose parents are in prison. And we need more talented teachers in troubled schools.

USA Freedom Corps will expand and improve the good efforts of AmeriCorps and Senior Corps to recruit more than 200,000 new volunteers.

And America needs citizens to extend the compassion of our country to every part of the world, so we will renew the promise of the Peace Corps, double its volunteers over the next five years and ask it to join a new effort to encourage development and education and opportunity in the Islamic world.

This time of adversity offers a unique moment of opportunity, a moment we must seize to change our culture. Through the gathering momentum of millions of acts of service and decency and kindness, I know we can overcome evil with greater good.

And we have a great opportunity during this time of war to lead the world toward the values that will bring lasting peace. All fathers and mothers, in all societies, want their children to be educated and live free from poverty and violence.

No people on Earth yearn to be oppressed or aspire to servitude or eagerly await the midnight knock of the secret police.

If anyone doubts this, let them look to Afghanistan, where the Islamic street greeted the fall of tyranny with song and celebration. Let the skeptics look to Islam's own rich history, with its centuries of learning and tolerance and progress.

America will lead by defending liberty and justice because they are right and true and unchanging for all people everywhere.

No nation owns these aspirations, and no nation is exempt from them. We have no intention of imposing our culture, but America will always stand firm for the nonnegotiable demands of human dignity: the rule of law, limits on the power of the state, respect for women, private property, free speech, equal justice and religious tolerance.

America will take the side of brave men and women who advocate these values around the world — including the Islamic world — because we have a greater objective than eliminating threats and containing resentment.

We seek a just and peaceful world beyond the war on terror.

In this moment of opportunity, a common danger is erasing old rivalries. America is working with Russia, and China and India in ways we never have before to achieve peace and prosperity. In every region, free markets and free trade and free societies are proving their power to lift lives. Together with friends and allies from Europe to Asia, and Africa to Latin America, we will demonstrate that the forces of terror cannot stop the momentum of freedom.

The last time I spoke here, I expressed the hope that life would return to normal.

In some ways it has. In others it never will. Those of us who have lived through these challenging times have been changed by them. We've come to know truths that we will never question: Evil is real, and it must be opposed.

Beyond all differences of race or creed, we are one country, mourning together and facing danger together.

Deep in the American character there is honor, and it is stronger than cynicism. And many have discovered again that even in tragedy — especially in tragedy — God is near.

In a single instant, we realized that this will be a decisive decade in the history of liberty, that we have been called to a unique role in human events. Rarely has the world faced a choice more clear or consequential.

Our enemies send other people's children on missions of suicide and murder. They embrace tyranny and death as a cause and a creed. We stand for a different choice, made long ago, on the day of our founding. We affirm it again today. We choose freedom and the dignity of every life.

Steadfast in our purpose, we now press on. We have known freedom's price. We have shown freedom's power. And in this great conflict, my fellow Americans, we will see freedom's victory.

We Fight for a Just Peace

In every corner of America, the words "West Point" command immediate respect. This place where the Hudson River bends is more than a fine institution of learning. The United States Military Academy is the guardian of values that have shaped the soldiers who have shaped the history of the world.

A few of you have followed in the path of the perfect West Point graduate, Robert E. Lee, who never received a single demerit in four years. Some of you followed in the path of the imperfect graduate, Ulysses S. Grant, who had his fair share of demerits, and said the happiest day of his life was "the day I left West Point." During my college years I guess you could say I was ... During my college years I guess you could say I was a Grant man.

You walk in the tradition of Eisenhower and MacArthur, Patton and Bradley - the commanders who saved a civilization. And you walk in the tradition of second lieutenants who did the same, by fighting and dying on distant battlefields.

Graduates of this academy have brought creativity and courage to every field of endeavor. West Point produced the chief engineer of the Panama Canal, the mind behind the Manhattan Project, the first American to walk in space. This fine institution gave us the man they say invented baseball, and other young men over the years who perfected the game of football.

You know this, but many in America don't — George C. Marshall, a VMI graduate, is said to have given this order: "I want an officer for a secret and dangerous mission. I want

35

a West Point football player."

As you leave here today, I know there's one thing you'll never miss about this place: Being a plebe. But even a plebe at West Point is made to feel he or she has some standing in the world. I'm told that plebes, when asked whom they out-rank, are required to answer this: "Sir, the Superintendent's dog — the Commandant's cat, and all the admirals in the whole damn Navy." I probably won't be sharing that with the Secretary of the Navy.

West Point is guided by tradition, and in honor of the "Golden Children of the Corps," — I will observe one of the traditions you cherish most. As the Commander-in-Chief, I hereby grant amnesty to all cadets who are on restriction for minor conduct offenses. Those of you in the end zone might have cheered a little early. Because, you see, I'm going to let General Lennox define exactly what "minor" means.

Every West Point class is commissioned to the Armed Forces. Some West Point classes are also commissioned by history, to take part in a great new calling for their country. Speaking here to the class of 1942 — six months after Pearl Harbor — General Marshall said, "We're determined that before the sun sets on this terrible struggle, our flag will be recognized throughout the world as a symbol of freedom on the one hand, and of overwhelming power on the other."

Officers graduating that year helped fulfill that mission, defeating Japan and Germany, and then reconstructing those nations as allies. West Point graduates of the 1940s saw the rise of a deadly new challenge — the challenge of imperial communism — and opposed it from Korea to Berlin, to Viet-nam, and in the Cold War, from beginning to end. And as the sun set on their struggle, many of those West Point offic-ers lived to see a world transformed.

History has also issued its call to your generation. In your last year, America was attacked by a ruthless and re-sourceful enemy. You graduate from this Academy in a time of war, taking your place in an American military that is powerful and is honorable. Our war on terror is only begun, but in Afghanistan it was begun well.

I am proud of the men and women who have fought on my orders. America is profoundly grateful for all who serve the cause of freedom, and for all who have given their lives in its defense. This nation respects and trusts our military, and we are confident in your victories to come.

This war will take many turns we cannot predict. Yet I am certain of this: Wherever we carry it, the American flag will stand not only for our power, but for freedom. Our nation's cause has always been larger than our nation's defense. We fight, as we always fight, for a just peace — a peace that favors human liberty. We will defend the peace against threats from terrorists and tyrants. We will preserve the peace by building good relations among the great powers. And we will extend the peace by encouraging free and open societies on every continent.

Building this just peace is America's opportunity, and America's duty. From this day forward, it is your challenge, as well, and we will meet this challenge together. You will wear the uniform of a great and unique country. America has no empire to extend or utopia to establish. We wish for others only what we wish for ourselves — safety from violence, the rewards of liberty, and the hope for a better life.

In defending the peace, we face a threat with no precedent. Enemies in the past needed great armies and great industrial capabilities to endanger the American people and our nation. The attacks of September the 11th required a few hundred thousand dollars in the hands of a few dozen evil and deluded men. All of the chaos and suffering they caused came at much less than the cost of a single tank. The dangers have not passed. This government and the American people are on watch, we are ready, because we know the terrorists have more money and more men and more plans.

The gravest danger to freedom lies at the perilous cross-roads of radicalism and technology. When the spread of chemical and biological and nuclear weapons, along with ballistic missile technology — when that occurs, even weak states and small groups could attain a catastrophic power to strike great nations. Our enemies have declared this very intention, and have been caught seeking these terrible weapons. They want the capability to blackmail us, or to harm us, or to harm our friends — and we will oppose them with all our power.

For much of the last century, America's defense relied on the Cold War doctrines of deterrence and containment. In some cases, those strategies still apply. But new threats also require new thinking. Deterrence — the promise of massive retaliation against nations — means nothing against shadowy terrorist networks with no nation or citizens to defend. Containment is not possible when unbalanced dictators with weapons of mass destruction can deliver those weapons on missiles or secretly provide them to terrorist allies.

We cannot defend America and our friends by hoping for the best. We cannot put our faith in the word of tyrants, who solemnly sign nonproliferation treaties, and then systemically break them. If we wait for threats to fully materialize, we will have waited too long.

Homeland defense and missile defense are part of stronger security, and they're essential priorities for America. Yet the war on terror will not be won on the defensive. We must take the battle to the enemy, disrupt his plans, and confront the worst threats before they emerge. In the world we have entered, the only path to safety is the path of action. And this nation will act.

Our security will require the best intelligence, to reveal threats hidden in caves and growing in laboratories. Our security will require modernizing domestic agencies such as the FBI, so they're prepared to act, and act quickly, against danger. Our security will require transforming the military you will lead — a military that must be ready to strike at a moment's notice in any dark corner of the world. And our security will require all Americans to be forward-looking and resolute, to be ready for preemptive action when necessary to defend our liberty and to defend our lives.

The work ahead is difficult. The choices we will face are complex. We must uncover terror cells in 60 or more countries, using every tool of finance, intelligence and law enforcement. Along with our friends and allies, we must oppose proliferation and confront regimes that sponsor terror, as each case requires. Some nations need military training to fight terror, and we'll provide it. Other nations oppose terror, but tolerate the hatred that leads to terror — and that must change. We will send diplomats where they are needed, and we will send you, our soldiers, where you're needed.

All nations that decide for aggression and terror will pay a price. We will not leave the safety of America and the peace of the planet at the mercy of a few mad terrorists and tyrants. We will lift this dark threat from our country and from the world.

Because the war on terror will require resolve and patience, it will also require firm moral purpose. In this way our struggle is similar to the Cold War. Now, as then, our enemies are totalitarians, holding a creed of power with no place for human dignity. Now, as then, they seek to impose a joyless conformity, to control every life and all of life.

America confronted imperial communism in many different ways — diplomatic, economic, and military. Yet moral clarity was essential to our victory in the Cold War. When leaders like John F. Kennedy and Ronald Reagan refused to gloss over the brutality of tyrants, they gave hope to prisoners and dissidents and exiles, and rallied free nations to a great cause.

Some worry that it is somehow undiplomatic or impolite to speak the language of right and wrong. I disagree. Different circumstances require different methods, but not different moralities. Moral truth is the same in every culture, in every time, and in every place. Targeting innocent civilians for murder is always and everywhere wrong. Brutality against women is always and everywhere wrong. There can be no neutrality between justice and cruelty, between the innocent and the guilty. We are in a conflict between good and evil, and America will call evil by its name. By confronting evil and lawless regimes, we do not create a problem, we reveal a problem. And we will lead the world in opposing it.

As we defend the peace, we also have an historic opportunity to preserve the peace. We have our best chance since the rise of the nation state in the 17th century to build a world where the great powers compete in peace instead of prepare for war. The history of the last century, in particular, was dominated by a series of destructive national rivalries that left battlefields and graveyards across the Earth. Germany fought France, the Axis fought the Allies, and then the East fought the West, in proxy wars and tense standoffs, against a backdrop of nuclear Armageddon.

Competition between great nations is inevitable, but armed conflict in our world is not. More and more, civilized nations find ourselves on the same side — united by common dangers of terrorist violence and chaos. America has, and intends to keep, military strengths beyond challenge — thereby, making the destabilizing arms races of other eras pointless, and limiting rivalries to trade and other pursuits of peace.

Today the great powers are also increasingly united by common values, instead of divided by conflicting ideologies. The United States, Japan and our Pacific friends, and now all of Europe, share a deep commitment to human freedom, embodied in strong alliances such as NATO. And the tide of liberty is rising in many other nations.

Generations of West Point officers planned and practiced for battles with Soviet Russia. I've just returned from a new Russia, now a country reaching toward democracy, and our partner in the war against terror. Even in China, leaders are discovering that economic freedom is the only lasting source of national wealth. In time, they will find that social and political freedom is the only true source of national greatness.

When the great powers share common values, we are better able to confront serious regional conflicts together, better able to cooperate in preventing the spread of violence or economic chaos. In the past, great power rivals took sides in difficult regional problems, making divisions deeper and more complicated. Today, from the Middle East to South Asia, we are gathering broad international coalitions to increase the pressure for peace. We must build strong and great power relations when times are good; to help manage crisis when times are bad. America needs partners to preserve the peace, and we will work with every nation that shares this noble goal.

And finally, America stands for more than the absence of war. We have a great opportunity to extend a just peace, by replacing poverty, repression, and resentment around the world with hope of a better day. Through most of history, poverty was persistent, inescapable, and almost universal. In the last few decades, we've seen nations from Chile to South Korea build modern economies and freer societies, lifting millions of people out of despair and want. And there's no mystery to this achievement.

The 20th century ended with a single surviving model of human progress, based on nonnegotiable demands of human dignity, the rule of law, limits on the power of the state, respect for women and private property and free speech and equal justice and religious tolerance. America cannot impose this vision — yet we can support and reward governments that make the right choices for their own people. In our development aid, in our diplomatic efforts, in our international broadcasting, and in our educational assistance, the United States will promote moderation and tolerance and human rights. And we will defend the peace that makes all progress possible.

When it comes to the common rights and needs of men and women, there is no clash of civilizations. The requirements of freedom apply fully to Africa and Latin America and the entire Islamic world. The peoples of the Islamic nations want and deserve the same freedoms and opportunities as people in every nation. And their governments should listen to their hopes.

A truly strong nation will permit legal avenues of dissent for all groups that pursue their aspirations without violence. An advancing nation will pursue economic reform, to unleash the great entrepreneurial energy of its people. A thriving nation will respect the rights of women, because no society can prosper while denying opportunity to half its citizens. Mothers and fathers and children across the Islamic world, and all the world, share the same fears and aspirations. In poverty, they struggle. In tyranny, they suffer. And as we saw in Afghanistan, in liberation they celebrate.

America has a greater objective than controlling threats and containing resentment. We will work for a just and peaceful world beyond the war on terror.

The bicentennial class of West Point now enters this drama. With all in the United States Army, you will stand between your fellow citizens and grave danger. You will help establish a peace that allows millions around the world to live in liberty and to grow in prosperity. You will face times of calm, and times of crisis. And every test will find you prepared — because you're the men and women of West Point. You leave here marked by the character of this Academy, carrying with you the highest ideals of our nation.

Toward the end of his life, Dwight Eisenhower recalled the first day he stood on the plain at West Point. "The feeling came over me," he said, "that the expression 'the United States of America' would now and henceforth mean something different than it had ever before. From here on, it would be the nation I would be serving, not myself."

Today, your last day at West Point, you begin a life of service in a career unlike any other. You've answered a calling to hardship and purpose, to risk and honor. At the end of every day you will know that you have faithfully done your duty. May you always bring to that duty the high standards of this great American institution. May you always be worthy of the long gray line that stretches two centuries behind you.

On behalf of the nation, I congratulate each one of you for the commission you've earned and for the credit you bring to the United States of America. May God bless you all.

Declaration of War on Iraqi Regime

Address to the United Nations
September 12, 2002

We meet one year and one day after a terrorist attack brought grief to my country and brought grief to many citizens of our world.

Yesterday we remembered the innocent lives taken that terrible morning. Today we turn to the urgent duty of protecting other lives without illusion and without fear.

We've accomplished much in the last year in Afghanistan and beyond. We have much yet to do in Afghanistan and beyond. Many nations represented here have joined in the fight against global terror and the people of the United States are grateful.

The United Nations was born in the hope that survived a world war, the hope of a world moving toward justice, escaping old patterns of conflict and fear. The founding members resolved that the peace of the world must never again be destroyed by the will and wickedness of any man.

We created a United Nations Security Council so that, unlike the League of Nations, our deliberations would be more than talk, our resolutions would be more than wishes. After generations of deceitful dictators and broken treaties and squandered lives, we've dedicated ourselves to standards of human dignity shared by all and to a system of security defended by all.

Today, these standards and this security are challenged.

Our commitment to human dignity is challenged by persistent poverty and raging disease. The suffering is great. And our responsibilities are clear. The United States is joining with the world to supply aid where it reaches people and lifts up lives, to extend trade and the prosperity it brings, and to bring medical care where it is desperately needed. As a symbol of our commitment to human dignity. The United States will return to UNESCO.

This organization has been reformed, and America will participate fully in its mission to advance human rights and tolerance and learning. Our common security is challenged by regional conflicts, ethnic and religious strife that is ancient, but not inevitable.

In the Middle East there can be no peace for either side without freedom for both sides.

America stands committed to an independent and democratic Palestine, living side-by-side with Israel in peace and security. Like all other people, Palestinians deserve a government that serves their interests and listens to their voices. My nation will continue to encourage all parties to step up to their responsibilities as we seek a just and comprehensive settlement to the conflict.

Above all, our principles and our security are challenged today by outlaw groups and regimes that accept no law of morality and have no limit to their violent ambitions. In the attacks on America a year ago, we saw the destructive intentions of our enemies. This threat hides within many nations, including my own.

In cells, in camps, terrorists are plotting further destruction and building new bases for their war against civilization. And our greatest fear is that terrorists will find a shortcut to their mad ambitions when an outlaw regime supplies them with the technologies to kill on a massive scale. In one place and one regime, we find all these dangers in their most lethal and aggressive forms, exactly the kind of aggressive threat the United Nations was born to confront.

Twelve years ago, Iraq invaded Kuwait without provocation. And the regime's forces were poised to continue their march to seize other countries and their resources. Had

Saddam Hussein been appeased instead of stopped, he would have endangered the peace and stability of the world. Yet this aggression was stopped by the might of coalition forces and the will of the United Nations.

To suspend hostilities, to spare himself, Iraq's dictator accepted a series of commitments. The terms were clear to him and to all, and he agreed to prove he is complying with every one of those obligations. He has proven instead only his contempt for the United Nations and for all his pledges. By breaking every pledge, by his deceptions and by his cruelties, Saddam Hussein has made the case against himself.

In 1991, Security Council Resolution 688 demanded that the Iraqi regime cease at once the repression of its own people, including the systematic repression of minorities, which the council said threatened international peace and security in the region. This demand goes ignored.

Last year, the U.N. Commission on Human Rights found that Iraq continues to commit extremely grave violations of human rights and that the regime's repression is all-pervasive.

Tens of thousands of political opponents and ordinary citizens have been subjected to arbitrary arrest and imprisonment, summary execution and torture by beating and burning, electric shock, starvation, mutilation and rape.

Wives are tortured in front of their husbands; children in the presence of their parents; and all of these horrors concealed from the world by the apparatus of a totalitarian state.

In 1991, the U.N. Security Council, through Resolutions 686 and 687, demanded that Iraq return all prisoners from Kuwait and other lands. Iraq's regime agreed. It broke this promise.

Last year, the Secretary General's high-level coordinator for this issue reported that Kuwaiti, Saudi, Indian, Syrian, Lebanese, Iranian, Egyptian, Bahraini and Armeni nationals remain unaccounted for; more than 600 people. One

American pilot is among them.

In 1991, the U.N. Security Council through Resolution 687 demanded that Iraq renounce all involvement with terrorism and permit no terrorist organizations to operate in Iraq.

Iraq's regime agreed that broke this promise.

In violation of Security Council Resolution 1373, Iraq continues to shelter and support terrorist organizations that direct violence against Iran, Israel and Western governments. Iraqi dissidents abroad are targeted for murder.

In 1993, Iraq attempted to assassinate the Amir of Kuwait and a former American president. Iraq's government openly praised the attacks of September 11. And Al Qaeda terrorists escaped from Afghanistan and are known to be in Iraq.

In 1991, the Iraqi regime agreed destroy and stop developing all weapons of mass destruction and long range missiles and to prove to the world it has done so by complying with rigorous inspections.

Iraq has broken every aspect of this fundamental pledge.

From 1991 to 1995, the Iraqi regime said it had no biological weapons. After a senior official in its weapons program defected and exposed this lie, the regime admitted to producing tens of thousands of liters of anthrax and other deadly biological agents for use with scud warheads, aerial bombs and aircraft spray tanks.

U.N. inspectors believe Iraq has produced two to four times the amount of biological agents it declared and has failed to account for more than three metric tons of material that could be used to produce biological weapons. Right now, Iraq is expanding and improving facilities that were used for the production of biological weapons.

United Nations' inspections also reviewed that Iraq like maintains stockpiles of VX, mustard and other chemical agents, and that the regime is rebuilding and expanding facilities capable of producing chemical weapons.

And in 1995, after four years of deception, Iraq finally admitted it had a crash nuclear weapons program prior to the Gulf War.

We know now, were it not for that war, the regime in Iraq would likely have possessed a nuclear weapon no later than 1993.

Today, Iraq continues to withhold important information about its nuclear program, weapons design, procurement logs, experiment data, and accounting of nuclear materials and documentation of foreign assistance. Iraq employs capable nuclear scientists and technicians. It retains physical infrastructure needed to build a nuclear weapon.

Iraq has made several attempts to buy high-strength aluminum tubes used to enrich uranium for a nuclear weapon. Should Iraq acquire fissile material, it would be able to build a nuclear weapon within a year.

And Iraq's state-controlled media has reported numerous meetings between Saddam Hussein and his nuclear scientists, leaving little doubt about his continued appetite for these weapons.

Iraq also possesses a force of SCUD type missiles with ranges beyond the 150 kilometers permitted by the U.N. Work at testing and production facilities shows that Iraq is building more long range missiles that can inflict mass death throughout the region.

In 1990, after Iraq's invasion of Kuwait, the world imposed economic sanctions on Iraq. Those sanctions were maintained after the war to compel the regime's compliance with Security Council Resolutions.

In time, Iraq was allowed to use oil revenues to buy food. Saddam Hussein has subverted this program, working around the sanctions to buy missile technology and military materials. He blames the suffering of Iraq's people on the United Nations, even as he uses his oil wealth to build lavish palaces for himself and to buy arms for his country.

By refusing to comply with his own agreements, he bears full guilt for the hunger and misery of innocent Iraqi citizens. In 1991, Iraq promised U.N. inspectors immediate and unrestricted access to verify Iraq's commitment to rid itself of weapons of mass destruction and long range missiles. Iraq broke this promise, spending seven years deceiving, evading and harassing U.N. inspectors before ceasing cooperation entirely.

Just months after the 1991 cease-fire, the Security Council twice renewed its demand that the Iraqi regime cooperate fully with inspectors, condemning Iraq's serious violations of its obligations. The Security Council again renewed that demand in 1994, and twice more in 1996, deploring Iraq's clear violations of its obligations.

The Security Council renewed its demand three more times in 1997, citing flagrant violations, and three more times in 1998, calling Iraq's behavior totally unacceptable. And in 1999, the demand was renewed yet again.

As we meet today, it's been almost four years since the last U.N. inspector set foot in Iraq — four years for the Iraqi regime to plan and to build and to test behind the cloak of secrecy. We know that Saddam Hussein pursued weapons of mass murder even when inspectors were in his country. Are we to assume that he stopped when they left?

The history, the logic and the facts lead to one conclusion: Saddam Hussein regime is a grave and gathering danger.

To suggest otherwise is to hope against the evidence. To assume this regime's good faith is to bet the lives of millions and the peace of the world in a reckless gamble, and this is a risk we must not take.

Delegates to the General Assembly, we have been more than patient. We've tried sanctions. We've tried the carrot of oil for food and the stick of coalition military strikes. But

Saddam Hussein has defied all these efforts and continues to develop weapons of mass destruction.

The first time we may be completely certain he has nuclear weapons is when, God forbid, he uses one. We owe it to all our citizens to do everything in our power to prevent that day from coming.

The conduct of the Iraqi regime is a threat to the authority of the United Nations and a threat to peace. Iraq has answered a decade of U.N. demands with a decade of defiance. All the world now faces a test, and the United Nations a difficult and defining moment.

Are Security Council resolutions to be honored and enforced or cast aside without consequence?

Will the United Nations serve the purpose of its founding or will it be irrelevant?

The United States help found the United Nations. We want the United Nations to be effective and respectful and successful. We want the resolutions of the world's most important multilateral body to be enforced. And right now those resolutions are being unilaterally subverted by the Iraqi regime.

Our partnership of nations can meet the test before us by making clear what we now expect of the Iraqi regime.

If the Iraqi regime wishes peace, it will immediately and unconditionally forswear, disclose and remove or destroy all weapons of mass destruction, long-range missiles and all related material.

If the Iraqi regime wishes peace, it will immediately end all support for terrorism and act to suppress it — as all states are required to do by U.N. Security Council resolutions.

If the Iraqi regime wishes peace, it will cease persecution of its civilian population, including Shi'a, Sunnis, Kurds, Turkemens and others — again, as required by Security Council resolutions.

If the Iraqi regime wishes peace, it will release or account for all Gulf War personnel whose fate is still unknown.

It will return the remains of any who are deceased, return stolen property, accept liability for losses resulting from the invasion of Kuwait and fully cooperate with international efforts to resolve these issues as required by Security Council resolutions.

If the Iraqi regime wishes peace, it will immediately end all illicit trade outside the oil-for-food program. It will accept U.N. administration of funds from that program to ensure that the money is used fairly and promptly for the benefit of the Iraqi people.

If all these steps are taken, it will signal a new openness and accountability in Iraq and it could open the prospect of the United Nations helping to build a government that represents all Iraqis, a government based on respect for human rights, economic liberty and internationally supervised elections.

The United States has no quarrel with the Iraqi people. They've suffered too long in silent captivity. Liberty for the Iraqi people is a great moral cause and a great strategic goal.

The people of Iraq deserve it. The security of all nations requires it. Free societies do not intimidate through cruelty and conquest. And open societies do not threaten the world with mass murder. The United States supports political and economic liberty in a unified Iraq.

We can harbor no illusions, and that's important today to remember. Saddam Hussein attacked Iran in 1980 and Kuwait in 1990. He's fired ballistic missiles at Iran and Saudi Arabia, Bahrain and Israel. His regime once ordered the killing of every person between the ages of 15 and 70 in certain Kurdish villages in northern Iraq. He has gassed many Iranians and 40 Iraqi villages.

My nation will work with the U.N. Security Council to meet our common challenge. If Iraq's regime defies us again, the world must move deliberately, decisively to hold Iraq to account. We will work with the U.N. Security Council for the necessary resolutions.

But the purposes of the United States should not be doubted. The Security Council resolutions will be enforced, the just demands of peace and security will be met or action will be unavoidable and a regime that has lost its legitimacy will also lose its power.

Events can turn in one of two ways. If we fail to act in the face of danger, the people of Iraq will continue to live in brutal submission. The regime will have new power to bully and dominate and conquer its neighbors, condemning the Middle East to more years of bloodshed and fear. The regime will remain unstable — the region will remain unstable, with little hope of freedom and isolated from the progress of our times.

With every step the Iraqi regime takes toward gaining and deploying the most terrible weapons, our own options to confront that regime will narrow. And if an emboldened regime were to supply these weapons to terrorists allies, then the attacks of September 11 would be a prelude to far greater horrors.

If we meet our responsibilities, if we overcome this danger, we can arrive at a very different future. The people of Iraq can shake off their captivity. They can one day join a democratic Afghanistan and a democratic Palestine inspiring reforms throughout the Muslim world. These nations can show by their example that honest government and respect for women and the great Islamic tradition of learning can triumph in the Middle East and beyond. And we will show that the promise of the United Nations can be fulfilled in our time.

Neither of these outcomes is certain. Both have been set before us. We must choose between a world of fear and a world of progress. We cannot stand by and do nothing while dangers gather. We must stand up for our security and for the permanent rights and the hopes of mankind.

By heritage and by choice, the United States of America will make that stand. And, delegates to the United Nations, you have the power to make that stand, as well.

Thank you very much.

2003 State of the Union

Joint Session of Congress
January 28, 2002

You and I serve our country in a time of great consequence. During this session of Congress, we have the duty to reform domestic programs vital to our country; we have the opportunity to save millions of lives abroad from a terrible disease. We will work for a prosperity that is broadly shared, and we will answer every danger and every enemy that threatens the American people.

In all these days of promise and days of reckoning, we can be confident. In a whirlwind of change and hope and peril, our faith is sure, our resolve is firm, and our union is strong.

This country has many challenges. We will not deny, we will not ignore, we will not pass along our problems to other Congresses, to other presidents, and other generations. We will confront them with focus and clarity and courage.

During the last two years, we have seen what can be accomplished when we work together. To lift the standards of our public schools, we achieved historic education reform — which must now be carried out in every school and in every classroom, so that every child in America can read and learn and succeed in life. To protect our country, we reorganized our government and created the Department of Homeland Security, which is mobilizing against the threats of a new era. To bring our economy out of recession, we delivered the largest tax relief in a generation. To insist on integrity in American business we passed tough reforms, and we are holding corporate criminals to account.

Some might call this a good record; I call it a good start.

Tonight I ask the House and Senate to join me in the next bold steps to serve our fellow citizens.

Our first goal is clear: We must have an economy that grows fast enough to employ every man and woman who seeks a job. After recession, terrorist attacks, corporate scandals and stock market declines, our economy is recovering — yet it's not growing fast enough, or strongly enough. With unemployment rising, our nation needs more small businesses to open, more companies to invest and expand, more employers to put up the sign that says, "Help Wanted."

Jobs are created when the economy grows; the economy grows when Americans have more money to spend and invest; and the best and fairest way to make sure Americans have that money is not to tax it away in the first place.

I am proposing that all the income tax reductions set for 2004 and 2006 be made permanent and effective this year. And under my plan, as soon as I sign the bill, this extra money will start showing up in workers' paychecks. Instead of gradually reducing the marriage penalty, we should do it now. Instead of slowly raising the child credit to $1,000, we should send the checks to American families now.

The tax relief is for everyone who pays income taxes — and it will help our economy immediately: 92 million Americans will keep, this year, an average of almost $1,000 more of their own money. A family of four with an income of $40,000 would see their federal income taxes fall from $1,178 to $45 per year. Our plan will improve the bottom line for more than 23 million small businesses.

You, the Congress, have already passed all these reductions, and promised them for future years. If this tax relief is good for Americans three, or five, or seven years from now, it is even better for Americans today.

We should also strengthen the economy by treating investors equally in our tax laws. It's fair to tax a company's profits. It is not fair to again tax the shareholder on the same profits. To boost investor confidence, and to help the nearly 10 million senior who receive dividend income, I ask you to end the unfair double taxation of dividends.

Lower taxes and greater investment will help this economy expand. More jobs mean more taxpayers, and higher revenues to our government. The best way to address the deficit and move toward a balanced budget is to encourage economic growth, and to show some spending discipline in Washington, D.C.

We must work together to fund only our most important priorities. I will send you a budget that increases discretionary spending by 4 percent next year — about as much as the average family's income is expected to grow. And that is a good benchmark for us. Federal spending should not rise any faster than the paychecks of American families.

A growing economy and a focus on essential priorities will also be crucial to the future of Social Security. As we continue to work together to keep Social Security sound and reliable, we must offer younger workers a chance to invest in retirement accounts that they will control and they will own.

Our second goal is high quality, affordable health care for all Americans. The American system of medicine is a model of skill and innovation, with a pace of discovery that is adding good years to our lives. Yet for many people, medical care costs too much — and many have no coverage at all. These problems will not be solved with a nationalized health care system that dictates coverage and rations care.

Instead, we must work toward a system in which all Americans have a good insurance policy, choose their own doctors, and seniors and low-income Americans receive the help they need. Instead of bureaucrats and trial lawyers and HMOs, we must put doctors and nurses and patients back in charge of American medicine.

Health care reform must begin with Medicare; Medicare is the binding commitment of a caring society. We must renew that commitment by giving seniors access to preventive medicine and new drugs that are transforming health care in America.

Seniors happy with the current Medicare system should be able to keep their coverage just the way it is. (Applause.) And just like you — the members of Congress, and your staffs, and other federal employees — all seniors should have the choice of a health care plan that provides prescription drugs.

My budget will commit an additional $400 billion over the next decade to reform and strengthen Medicare. Leaders of both political parties have talked for years about strengthening Medicare. I urge the members of this new Congress to act this year.

To improve our health care system, we must address one of the prime causes of higher cost, the constant threat that physicians and hospitals will be unfairly sued. Because of excessive litigation, everybody pays more for health care, and many parts of America are losing fine doctors. No one has ever been healed by a frivolous lawsuit. I urge the Congress to pass medical liability reform.

Our third goal is to promote energy independence for our country, while dramatically improving the environment. I have sent you a comprehensive energy plan to promote energy efficiency and conservation, to develop cleaner technology, and to produce more energy at home. I have sent you Clear Skies legislation that mandates a 70 percent cut in air pollution from power plants over the next 15 years. I have sent you a Healthy Forests Initiative, to help prevent the catastrophic fires that devastate communities, kill wildlife, and burn away millions of acres of treasured forest.

I urge you to pass these measures, for the good of both our environment and our economy. Even more, I ask you to take a crucial step and protect our environment in ways that generations before us could not have imagined.

In this century, the greatest environmental progress will

come about not through endless lawsuits or command-and-control regulations, but through technology and innovation. Tonight I'm proposing $1.2 billion in research funding so that America can lead the world in developing clean, hydrogen-powered automobiles.

A single chemical reaction between hydrogen and oxygen generates energy, which can be used to power a car — producing only water, not exhaust fumes. With a new national commitment, our scientists and engineers will overcome obstacles to taking these cars from laboratory to showroom, so that the first car driven by a child born today could be powered by hydrogen, and pollution-free.

Join me in this important innovation to make our air significantly cleaner, and our country much less dependent on foreign sources of energy.

Our fourth goal is to apply the compassion of America to the deepest problems of America. For so many in our country — the homeless and the fatherless, the addicted — the need is great. Yet there's power, wonder-working power, in the goodness and idealism and faith of the American people.

Americans are doing the work of compassion every day — visiting prisoners, providing shelter for battered women, bringing companionship to lonely seniors. These good works deserve our praise; they deserve our personal support; and when appropriate, they deserve the assistance of the federal government.

I urge you to pass both my faith-based initiative and the Citizen Service Act, to encourage acts of compassion that can transform America, one heart and one soul at a time.

Last year, I called on my fellow citizens to participate in the USA Freedom Corps, which is enlisting tens of thousands of new volunteers across America. Tonight I ask Congress and the American people to focus the spirit of service and the resources of government on the needs of some of our most vulnerable citizens — boys and girls trying to grow up without guidance and attention, and children who have to go through a prison gate to be hugged by their mom or dad.

I propose a $450 million initiative to bring mentors to more than a million disadvantaged junior high students and children of prisoners. Government will support the training and recruiting of mentors; yet it is the men and women of America who will fill the need. One mentor, one person can change a life forever. And I urge you to be that one person.

Another cause of hopelessness is addiction to drugs. Addiction crowds out friendship, ambition, moral conviction, and reduces all the richness of life to a single destructive desire. As a government, we are fighting illegal drugs by cutting off supplies and reducing demand through anti-drug education programs. Yet for those already addicted, the fight against drugs is a fight for their own lives. Too many Americans in search of treatment cannot get it. So tonight I propose a new $600-million program to help an additional 300,000 Americans receive treatment over the next three years.

Our nation is blessed with recovery programs that do amazing work. One of them is found at the Healing Place Church in Baton Rouge, Louisiana. A man in the program said, "God does miracles in people's lives, and you never think it could be you." Tonight, let us bring to all Americans who struggle with drug addiction this message of hope: The miracle of recovery is possible, and it could be you.

By caring for children who need mentors, and for addicted men and women who need treatment, we are building a more welcoming society — a culture that values every life. And in this work we must not overlook the weakest among us. I ask you to protect infants at the very hour of their birth and end the practice of partial-birth abortion. And because no human life should be started or ended as the object of an experiment, I ask you to set a high standard for humanity, and pass a law against all human cloning.

The qualities of courage and compassion that we strive for in America also determine our conduct abroad. The American flag stands for more than our power and our interests. Our founders dedicated this country to the cause of human dignity, the rights of every person, and the possibilities of every life. This conviction leads us into the world to help the afflicted, and defend the peace, and confound the designs of evil men.

In Afghanistan, we helped liberate an oppressed people. And we will continue helping them secure their country, rebuild their society, and educate all their children — boys and girls. In the Middle East, we will continue to seek peace between a secure Israel and a democratic Palestine. Across the Earth, America is feeding the hungry — more than 60 percent of international food aid comes as a gift from the people of the United States. As our nation moves troops and builds alliances to make our world safer, we must also remember our calling as a blessed country is to make this world better.

Today, on the continent of Africa, nearly 30 million people have the AIDS virus — including 3 million children under the age 15. There are whole countries in Africa where more than one-third of the adult population carries the infection. More than 4 million require immediate drug treatment. Yet across that continent, only 50,000 AIDS victims — only 50,000 — are receiving the medicine they need.

Because the AIDS diagnosis is considered a death sentence, many do not seek treatment. Almost all who do are turned away. A doctor in rural South Africa describes his frustration. He says, "We have no medicines. Many hospitals tell people, you've got AIDS, we can't help you. Go home and die." In an age of miraculous medicines, no person should have to hear those words.

AIDS can be prevented. Anti-retroviral drugs can extend life for many years. And the cost of those drugs has dropped from $12,000 a year to under $300 a year — which places a tremendous possibility within our grasp. Ladies and gentlemen, seldom has history offered a greater opportunity to do so much for so many.

We have confronted, and will continue to confront, HIV/AIDS in our own country. And to meet a severe and urgent crisis abroad, tonight I propose the Emergency Plan for AIDS Relief — a work of mercy beyond all current international efforts to help the people of Africa. This comprehensive plan will prevent 7 million new AIDS infections, treat at least 2 million people with life-extending drugs, and provide humane care for millions of people suffering from AIDS, and for children orphaned by AIDS.

I ask the Congress to commit $15 billion over the next five years, including nearly $10 billion in new money, to turn the tide against AIDS in the most afflicted nations of Africa and the Caribbean.

This nation can lead the world in sparing innocent people from a plague of nature. And this nation is leading the world in confronting and defeating the man-made evil of international terrorism.

There are days when our fellow citizens do not hear news about the war on terror. There's never a day when I do not learn of another threat, or receive reports of operations in progress, or give an order in this global war against a scattered network of killers. The war goes on, and we are winning.

To date, we've arrested or otherwise dealt with many key commanders of al Qaeda. They include a man who directed logistics and funding for the September the 11th attacks; the chief of al Qaeda operations in the Persian Gulf, who planned the bombings of our embassies in East Africa and the USS Cole; an al Qaeda operations chief from Southeast Asia; a former director of al Qaeda's training camps in Afghanistan; a key al Qaeda operative in Europe; a major al Qaeda leader in Yemen. All told, more than 3,000 suspected terrorists have been arrested in many countries. Many others have met a different fate. Let's put it this way — they are no longer a problem to the United States and our friends and allies.

We are working closely with other nations to prevent further attacks. America and coalition countries have uncovered and stopped terrorist conspiracies targeting the American embassy in Yemen, the American embassy in Singapore, a Saudi military base, ships in the Straits of Hormuz and the Straits the Gibraltar. We've broken al Qaeda cells in Hamburg, Milan, Madrid, London, Paris, as well as, Buffalo, New York.

We have the terrorists on the run. We're keeping them on the run. One by one, the terrorists are learning the meaning of American justice.

As we fight this war, we will remember where it began — here, in our own country. This government is taking unprecedented measures to protect our people and defend our homeland. We've intensified security at the borders and ports of entry, posted more than 50,000 newly-trained federal screeners in airports, begun inoculating troops and first responders against smallpox, and are deploying the nation's first early warning network of sensors to detect biological attack. And this year, for the first time, we are beginning to field a defense to protect this nation against ballistic missiles.

I thank the Congress for supporting these measures. I ask you tonight to add to our future security with a major research and production effort to guard our people against bioterrorism, called Project Bioshield. The budget I send you will propose almost $6 billion to quickly make available effective vaccines and treatments against agents like anthrax, botulinum toxin, Ebola, and plague. We must assume that our enemies would use these diseases as weapons, and we must act before the dangers are upon us.

Since September the 11th, our intelligence and law enforcement agencies have worked more closely than ever to track and disrupt the terrorists. The FBI is improving its ability to analyze intelligence, and is transforming itself to meet new threats. Tonight, I am instructing the leaders of the FBI, the CIA, the Homeland Security, and the Department of Defense to develop a Terrorist Threat Integration Center, to merge and analyze all threat information in a single location. Our government must have the very best information possible, and we will use it to make sure the right people are in the right places to protect all our citizens. Our war against terror is a contest of will in which perseverance is power. In the ruins of two towers, at the western wall of the Pentagon, on a field in Pennsylvania, this nation made a pledge, and we renew that pledge tonight: Whatever the duration of this struggle, and whatever the difficulties, we will not permit the triumph of violence in the affairs of men — free people will set the course of history.

Today, the gravest danger in the war on terror, the gravest danger facing America and the world, is outlaw regimes that seek and possess nuclear, chemical, and biological weapons. These regimes could use such weapons for blackmail, terror, and mass murder. They could also give or sell those weapons to terrorist allies, who would use them without the least hesitation.

This threat is new; America's duty is familiar. Throughout the 20th century, small groups of men seized control of great nations, built armies and arsenals, and set out to dominate the weak and intimidate the world. In each case, their ambitions of cruelty and murder had no limit. In each case, the ambitions of Hitlerism, militarism, and communism were defeated by the will of free peoples, by the strength of great alliances, and by the might of the United States of America.

Now, in this century, the ideology of power and domination has appeared again, and seeks to gain the ultimate weapons of terror. Once again, this nation and all our friends are all that stand between a world at peace, and a world of chaos and constant alarm. Once again, we are called to defend the safety of our people, and the hopes of all mankind. And we accept this responsibility.

America is making a broad and determined effort to confront these dangers. We have called on the United Nations to fulfill its charter and stand by its demand that Iraq disarm. We're strongly supporting the International Atomic Energy Agency in its mission to track and control nuclear materials around the world. We're working with other governments to secure nuclear materials in the former Soviet Union, and to strengthen global treaties banning the production and shipment of missile technologies and weapons of mass destruction.

In all these efforts, however, America's purpose is more than to follow a process — it is to achieve a result: the end of terrible threats to the civilized world. All free nations have a stake in preventing sudden and catastrophic attacks. And we're asking them to join us, and many are doing so. Yet the course of this nation does not depend on the decisions of others. Whatever action is required, whenever action is necessary, I will defend the freedom and security of the American people.

Different threats require different strategies. In Iran, we continue to see a government that represses its people, pursues weapons of mass destruction, and supports terror. We also see Iranian citizens risking intimidation and death as they speak out for liberty and human rights and democracy. Iranians, like all people, have a right to choose their own government and determine their own destiny — and the United States supports their aspirations to live in freedom.

On the Korean Peninsula, an oppressive regime rules a people living in fear and starvation. Throughout the 1990s, the United States relied on a negotiated framework to keep

North Korea from gaining nuclear weapons. We now know that that regime was deceiving the world, and developing those weapons all along. And today the North Korean regime is using its nuclear program to incite fear and seek concessions. America and the world will not be blackmailed.

America is working with the countries of the region — South Korea, Japan, China, and Russia — to find a peaceful solution, and to show the North Korean government that nuclear weapons will bring only isolation, economic stagnation, and continued hardship. The North Korean regime will find respect in the world and revival for its people only when it turns away from its nuclear ambitions.

Our nation and the world must learn the lessons of the Korean Peninsula and not allow an even greater threat to rise up in Iraq. A brutal dictator, with a history of reckless aggression, with ties to terrorism, with great potential wealth, will not be permitted to dominate a vital region and threaten the United States.

Twelve years ago, Saddam Hussein faced the prospect of being the last casualty in a war he had started and lost. To spare himself, he agreed to disarm of all weapons of mass destruction. For the next 12 years, he systematically violated that agreement. He pursued chemical, biological, and nuclear weapons, even while inspectors were in his country. Nothing to date has restrained him from his pursuit of these weapons — not economic sanctions, not isolation from the civilized world, not even cruise missile strikes on his military facilities.

Almost three months ago, the United Nations Security Council gave Saddam Hussein his final chance to disarm. He has shown instead utter contempt for the United Nations, and for the opinion of the world. The 108 U.N. inspectors were sent to conduct — were not sent to conduct a scavenger hunt for hidden materials across a country the size of California. The job of the inspectors is to verify that Iraq's regime is disarming. It is up to Iraq to show exactly where it is hiding its banned weapons, lay those weapons out for the world to see, and destroy them as directed. Nothing like this has happened.

The United Nations concluded in 1999 that Saddam Hussein had biological weapons sufficient to produce over 25,000 liters of anthrax — enough doses to kill several million people. He hasn't accounted for that material. He's given no evidence that he has destroyed it.

The United Nations concluded that Saddam Hussein had materials sufficient to produce more than 38,000 liters of botulinum toxin — enough to subject millions of people to death by respiratory failure. He hadn't accounted for that material. He's given no evidence that he has destroyed it.

Our intelligence officials estimate that Saddam Hussein had the materials to produce as much as 500 tons of sarin, mustard and VX nerve agent. In such quantities, these chemical agents could also kill untold thousands. He's not accounted for these materials. He has given no evidence that he has destroyed them.

U.S. intelligence indicates that Saddam Hussein had upwards of 30,000 munitions capable of delivering chemical agents. Inspectors recently turned up 16 of them — despite Iraq's recent declaration denying their existence. Saddam Hussein has not accounted for the remaining 29,984 of these prohibited munitions. He's given no evidence that he has destroyed them.

From three Iraqi defectors we know that Iraq, in the late 1990s, had several mobile biological weapons labs. These are designed to produce germ warfare agents, and can be moved from place to a place to evade inspectors. Saddam Hussein has not disclosed these facilities. He's given no evidence that he has destroyed them.

The International Atomic Energy Agency confirmed in the 1990s that Saddam Hussein had an advanced nuclear weapons development program, had a design for a nuclear weapon and was working on five different methods of enriching uranium for a bomb. The British government has learned that Saddam Hussein recently sought significant quantities of uranium from Africa. Our intelligence sources tell us that he has attempted to purchase high-strength aluminum tubes suitable for nuclear weapons production. Saddam Hussein has not credibly explained these activities. He clearly has much to hide.

The dictator of Iraq is not disarming. To the contrary; he is deceiving. From intelligence sources we know, for instance, that thousands of Iraqi security personnel are at work hiding documents and materials from the U.N. inspectors, sanitizing inspection sites and monitoring the inspectors themselves. Iraqi officials accompany the inspectors in order to intimidate witnesses.

Iraq is blocking U-2 surveillance flights requested by the United Nations. Iraqi intelligence officers are posing as the scientists inspectors are supposed to interview. Real scientists have been coached by Iraqi officials on what to say. Intelligence sources indicate that Saddam Hussein has ordered that scientists who cooperate with U.N. inspectors in disarming Iraq will be killed, along with their families.

Year after year, Saddam Hussein has gone to elaborate lengths, spent enormous sums, taken great risks to build and keep weapons of mass destruction. But why? The only possible explanation, the only possible use he could have for those weapons, is to dominate, intimidate, or attack.

With nuclear arms or a full arsenal of chemical and biological weapons, Saddam Hussein could resume his ambitions of conquest in the Middle East and create deadly havoc in that region. And this Congress and the America people must recognize another threat. Evidence from intelligence sources, secret communications, and statements by people now in custody reveal that Saddam Hussein aids and protects terrorists, including members of al Qaeda. Secretly, and without fingerprints, he could provide one of his hidden weapons to terrorists, or help them develop their own.

Before September the 11th, many in the world believed that Saddam Hussein could be contained. But chemical agents, lethal viruses and shadowy terrorist networks are not easily contained. Imagine those 19 hijackers with other weapons and other plans — this time armed by Saddam Hussein. It would take one vial, one canister, one crate slipped into this country to bring a day of horror like none we have ever known. We will do everything in our power to make sure that that day never comes.

Some have said we must not act until the threat is imminent. Since when have terrorists and tyrants announced their intentions, politely putting us on notice before they strike? If this threat is permitted to fully and suddenly emerge, all actions, all words, and all recriminations would come too late. Trusting in the sanity and restraint of Saddam Hussein is not a strategy, and it is not an option.

The dictator who is assembling the world's most dangerous weapons has already used them on whole villages — leaving thousands of his own citizens dead, blind, or disfigured. Iraqi refugees tell us how forced confessions are obtained — by torturing children while their parents are made to watch. International human rights groups have catalogued other methods used in the torture chambers of Iraq: electric shock, burning with hot irons, dripping acid on the skin, mutilation with electric drills, cutting out tongues, and rape. If this is not evil, then evil has no meaning.

And tonight I have a message for the brave and oppressed people of Iraq: Your enemy is not surrounding your country — your enemy is ruling your country. And the day he and his regime are removed from power will be the day of your liberation.

The world has waited 12 years for Iraq to disarm.

America will not accept a serious and mounting threat to our country, and our friends and our allies. The United States will ask the U.N. Security Council to convene on February the 5th to consider the facts of Iraq's ongoing defiance of the world. Secretary of State Powell will present information and intelligence about Iraqi's legal — Iraq's illegal weapons programs, its attempt to hide those weapons from inspectors, and its links to terrorist groups.

We will consult. But let there be no misunderstanding: If Saddam Hussein does not fully disarm, for the safety of our people and for the peace of the world, we will lead a coalition to disarm him.

Tonight I have a message for the men and women who will keep the peace, members of the American Armed Forces: Many of you are assembling in or near the Middle East, and some crucial hours may lay ahead. In those hours, the success of our cause will depend on you. Your training has prepared you. Your honor will guide you. You believe in America, and America believes in you.

Sending Americans into battle is the most profound decision a President can make. The technologies of war have changed; the risks and suffering of war have not. For the brave Americans who bear the risk, no victory is free from sorrow. This nation fights reluctantly, because we know the cost and we dread the days of mourning that always come.

We seek peace. We strive for peace. And sometimes peace must be defended. A future lived at the mercy of terrible threats is no peace at all. If war is forced upon us, we will fight in a just cause and by just means — sparing, in every way we can, the innocent. And if war is forced upon us, we will fight with the full force and might of the United States military — and we will prevail.

And as we and our coalition partners are doing in Afghanistan, we will bring to the Iraqi people food and medicines and supplies — and freedom.

Many challenges, abroad and at home, have arrived in a single season. In two years, America has gone from a sense of invulnerability to an awareness of peril; from bitter division in small matters to calm unity in great causes. And we go forward with confidence, because this call of history has come to the right country.

Americans are a resolute people who have risen to every test of our time. Adversity has revealed the character of our country, to the world and to ourselves. America is a strong nation, and honorable in the use of our strength. We exercise power without conquest, and we sacrifice for the liberty of strangers.

Americans are a free people, who know that freedom is the right of every person and the future of every nation. The liberty we prize is not America's gift to the world, it is God's gift to humanity.

We Americans have faith in ourselves, but not in ourselves alone. We do not know — we do not claim to know all the ways of Providence, yet we can trust in them, placing our confidence in the loving God behind all of life, and all of history.

THE FUTURE OF IRAQ

AMERICAN ENTERPRISE INSTITUTE DINNER
FEBRUARY 26, 2003

I'm proud to be with the scholars, and the friends, and the supporters of the American Enterprise Institute. I want to thank you for overlooking my dress code violation. They were about to stop me at the door, but Irving Kristol said, "I know this guy, let him in."

Chris, thank you for your very kind introduction, and thank you for your leadership. I see many distinguished guests here tonight — members of my Cabinet, members of Congress, Justice Scalia, Justice Thomas, and so many respected writers and policy experts. I'm always happy to see your Senior Fellow, Dr. Lynne Cheney. Lynne is a wise and thoughtful commentator on history and culture, and a dear friend to Laura and me. I'm also familiar with the good work of her husband — You may remember him, the former director of my vice presidential search committee. Thank God Dick Cheney said yes.

Thanks for fitting me into the program tonight. I know I'm not the featured speaker. I'm just a warm-up act for Allan Meltzer. But I want to congratulate Dr. Meltzer for a lifetime of achievement, and for tonight's well-deserved honor. Congratulations.

At the American Enterprise Institute, some of the finest minds in our nation are at work on some of the greatest challenges to our nation. You do such good work that my administration has borrowed 20 such minds. I want to thank them for their service, but I also want to remind people that for 60 years, AEI scholars have made vital contributions to our country and to our government, and we are grateful for those

73

contributions.

We meet here during a crucial period in the history of our nation, and of the civilized world. Part of that history was written by others; the rest will be written by us. On a September morning, threats that had gathered for years, in secret and far away, led to murder in our country on a massive scale. As a result, we must look at security in a new way, because our country is a battlefield in the first war of the 21st century.

We learned a lesson: The dangers of our time must be confronted actively and forcefully, before we see them again in our skies and in our cities. And we set a goal: we will not allow the triumph of hatred and violence in the affairs of men.

Our coalition of more than 90 countries is pursuing the networks of terror with every tool of law enforcement and with military power. We have arrested, or otherwise dealt with, many key commanders of al Qaeda. Across the world, we are hunting down the killers one by one. We are winning. And we're showing them the definition of American justice. And we are opposing the greatest danger in the war on terror: outlaw regimes arming with weapons of mass destruction.

In Iraq, a dictator is building and hiding weapons that could enable him to dominate the Middle East and intimidate the civilized world — and we will not allow it. This same tyrant has close ties to terrorist organizations, and could supply them with the terrible means to strike this country — and America will not permit it. The danger posed by Saddam Hussein and his weapons cannot be ignored or wished away. The danger must be confronted. We hope that the Iraqi regime will meet the demands of the United Nations and disarm, fully and peacefully. If it does not, we are prepared to disarm Iraq by force. Either way, this danger will be removed.

The safety of the American people depends on ending

this direct and growing threat. Acting against the danger will also contribute greatly to the long-term safety and stability of our world. The current Iraqi regime has shown the power of tyranny to spread discord and violence in the Middle East. A liberated Iraq can show the power of freedom to transform that vital region, by bringing hope and progress into the lives of millions. America's interests in security, and America's belief in liberty, both lead in the same direction: to a free and peaceful Iraq.

The first to benefit from a free Iraq would be the Iraqi people, themselves. Today they live in scarcity and fear, under a dictator who has brought them nothing but war, and misery, and torture. Their lives and their freedom matter little to Saddam Hussein — but Iraqi lives and freedom matter greatly to us.

Bringing stability and unity to a free Iraq will not be easy. Yet that is no excuse to leave the Iraqi regime's torture chambers and poison labs in operation. Any future the Iraqi people choose for themselves will be better than the nightmare world that Saddam Hussein has chosen for them.

If we must use force, the United States and our coalition stand ready to help the citizens of a liberated Iraq. We will deliver medicine to the sick, and we are now moving into place nearly 3 million emergency rations to feed the hungry.

We'll make sure that Iraq's 55,000 food distribution sites, operating under the Oil For Food program, are stocked and open as soon as possible. The United States and Great Britain are providing tens of millions of dollars to the U.N. High Commission on Refugees, and to such groups as the World Food Program and UNICEF, to provide emergency aid to the Iraqi people.

We will also lead in carrying out the urgent and dangerous work of destroying chemical and biological weapons. We will provide security against those who try to spread chaos, or settle scores, or threaten the territorial integrity of Iraq. We will seek to protect Iraq's natural resources from sabotage by a dying regime, and ensure those resources are used for the benefit of the owners — the Iraqi people.

The United States has no intention of determining the precise form of Iraq's new government. That choice belongs to the Iraqi people. Yet, we will ensure that one brutal dictator is not replaced by another. All Iraqis must have a voice in the new government, and all citizens must have their rights protected.

Rebuilding Iraq will require a sustained commitment from many nations, including our own: we will remain in Iraq as long as necessary, and not a day more. America has made and kept this kind of commitment before — in the peace that followed a world war. After defeating enemies, we did not leave behind occupying armies, we left constitutions and parliaments. We established an atmosphere of safety, in which responsible, reform-minded local leaders could build lasting institutions of freedom. In societies that once bred fascism and militarism, liberty found a permanent home.

There was a time when many said that the cultures of Japan and Germany were incapable of sustaining democratic values. Well, they were wrong. Some say the same of Iraq today. They are mistaken. The nation of Iraq — with its proud heritage, abundant resources and skilled and educated people — is fully capable of moving toward democracy and living in freedom.

The world has a clear interest in the spread of democratic values, because stable and free nations do not breed the ideologies of murder. They encourage the peaceful pursuit of a better life. And there are hopeful signs of a desire for freedom in the Middle East. Arab intellectuals have called on Arab governments to address the "freedom gap" so their peoples can fully share in the progress of our times. Leaders in the region speak of a new Arab charter that champions internal reform, greater politics participation, economic openness, and free trade. And from Morocco to Bahrain and beyond, nations are taking genuine steps toward politics reform. A new regime in Iraq would serve as a dramatic and inspiring example of freedom for other nations in the region.

It is presumptuous and insulting to suggest that a whole region of the world — or the one-fifth of humanity that is Muslim — is somehow untouched by the most basic aspirations of life. Human cultures can be vastly different. Yet the human heart desires the same good things, everywhere on Earth. In our desire to be safe from brutal and bullying oppression, human beings are the same. In our desire to care for our children and give them a better life, we are the same. For these fundamental reasons, freedom and democracy will always and everywhere have greater appeal than the slogans of hatred and the tactics of terror.

Success in Iraq could also begin a new stage for Middle Eastern peace, and set in motion progress towards a truly democratic Palestinian state. The passing of Saddam Hussein's regime will deprive terrorist networks of a wealthy patron that pays for terrorist training, and offers rewards to families of suicide bombers. And other regimes will be given a clear warning that support for terror will not be tolerated.

Without this outside support for terrorism, Palestinians who are working for reform and long for democracy will be in a better position to choose new leaders. True leaders who strive for peace; true leaders who faithfully serve the people. A Palestinian state must be a reformed and peaceful state that abandons forever the use of terror.

For its part, the new government of Israel — as the terror threat is removed and security improves — will be expected to support the creation of a viable Palestinian state — and to work as quickly as possible toward a final status agreement. As progress is made toward peace, settlement activity in the occupied territories must end. And the Arab states will be expected to meet their responsibilities to oppose terrorism, to support the emergence of a peaceful and democratic Palestine, and state clearly they will live in peace with Israel.

The United States and other nations are working on a road map for peace. We are setting out the necessary conditions for progress toward the goal of two states, Israel and Palestine, living side by side in peace and security. It is the commitment of our government — and my personal commitment — to implement the road map and to reach that goal. Old patterns of conflict in the Middle East can be broken, if all concerned will let go of bitterness, hatred, and violence, and get on with the serious work of economic development, and political reform, and reconciliation. America will seize every opportunity in pursuit of peace. And the end of the present regime in Iraq would create such an opportunity.

In confronting Iraq, the United States is also showing our commitment to effective international institutions. We are a permanent member of the United Nations Security Council. We helped to create the Security Council. We believe in the Security Council — so much that we want its words to have meaning.

The global threat of proliferation of weapons of mass destruction cannot be confronted by one nation alone. The world needs today and will need tomorrow international bodies with the authority and the will to stop the spread of terror and chemical and biological and nuclear weapons. A threat to all must be answered by all. High-minded pronouncements against proliferation mean little unless the strongest nations are willing to stand behind them — and use force if necessary. After all, the United Nations was created, as Winston Churchill said, to "make sure that the force of right will, in the ultimate issue, be protected by the right of force."

Another resolution is now before the Security Council. If the council responds to Iraq's defiance with more excuses and delays, if all its authority proves to be empty, the United Nations will be severely weakened as a source of stability and order. If the members rise to this moment, then the Council will fulfill its founding purpose.

I've listened carefully, as people and leaders around the world have made known their desire for peace. All of us want peace. The threat to peace does not come from those who seek to enforce the just demands of the civilized world; the threat to peace comes from those who flout those demands. If we have to act, we will act to restrain the violent, and defend the cause of peace. And by acting, we will signal to outlaw regimes that in this new century, the boundaries of civilized behavior will be respected.

Protecting those boundaries carries a cost. If war is forced upon us by Iraq's refusal to disarm, we will meet an enemy who hides his military forces behind civilians, who has terrible weapons, who is capable of any crime. The dangers are real, as our soldiers, and sailors, airmen, and Marines fully understand. Yet, no military has ever been better prepared to meet these challenges.

Members of our Armed Forces also understand why they may be called to fight. They know that retreat before a dictator guarantees even greater sacrifices in the future. They know that America's cause is right and just: liberty for an oppressed people, and security for the American people. And I know something about these men and women who wear our uniform: they will complete every mission they are given with skill, and honor, and courage.

Much is asked of America in this year 2003. The work ahead is demanding. It will be difficult to help freedom take hold in a country that has known three decades of dictatorship, secret police, internal divisions, and war. It will be difficult to cultivate liberty and peace in the Middle East, after so many generations of strife. Yet, the security of our nation and the hope of millions depend on us, and Americans do not turn away from duties because they are hard. We have met great tests in other times, and we will meet the tests of our time.

We go forward with confidence, because we trust in the power of human freedom to change lives and nations. By the resolve and purpose of America, and of our friends and allies, we will make this an age of progress and liberty. Free people will set the course of history, and free people will keep the peace of the world.

MAJOR COMBAT OPERATIONS IN IRAQ HAVE ENDED

U.S.S. ABRAHAM LINCOLN, SAN DIEGO COAST
MAY 1, 2003

Admiral Kelly, Captain Card, officers and sailors of the USS Abraham Lincoln, my fellow Americans: Major combat operations in Iraq have ended. In the battle of Iraq, the United States and our allies have prevailed. And now our coalition is engaged in securing and reconstructing that country.

In this battle, we have fought for the cause of liberty, and for the peace of the world. Our nation and our coalition are proud of this accomplishment — yet, it is you, the members of the United States military, who achieved it. Your courage, your willingness to face danger for your country and for each other, made this day possible. Because of you, our nation is more secure. Because of you, the tyrant has fallen, and Iraq is free.

Operation Iraqi Freedom was carried out with a combination of precision and speed and boldness the enemy did not expect, and the world had not seen before. From distant bases or ships at sea, we sent planes and missiles that could destroy an enemy division, or strike a single bunker. Marines and soldiers charged to Baghdad across 350 miles of hostile ground, in one of the swiftest advances of heavy arms in history. You have shown the world the skill and the might of the American Armed Forces.

This nation thanks all the members of our coalition who joined in a noble cause. We thank the Armed Forces of the United Kingdom, Australia, and Poland, who shared in the hardships of war. We thank all the citizens of Iraq who welcomed our troops and joined in the liberation of their own country. And tonight, I have a special word for Secretary

Rumsfeld, for General Franks, and for all the men and women who wear the uniform of the United States: America is grateful for a job well done.

The character of our military through history — the daring of Normandy, the fierce courage of Iwo Jima, the decency and idealism that turned enemies into allies — is fully present in this generation. When Iraqi civilians looked into the faces of our servicemen and women, they saw strength and kindness and goodwill. When I look at the members of the United States military, I see the best of our country, and I'm honored to be your Commander-in-Chief.

In the images of falling statues, we have witnessed the arrival of a new era. For a hundred of years of war, culminating in the nuclear age, military technology was designed and deployed to inflict casualties on an ever-growing scale. In defeating Nazi Germany and Imperial Japan, Allied forces destroyed entire cities, while enemy leaders who started the conflict were safe until the final days. Military power was used to end a regime by breaking a nation.

Today, we have the greater power to free a nation by breaking a dangerous and aggressive regime. With new tactics and precision weapons, we can achieve military objectives without directing violence against civilians. No device of man can remove the tragedy from war; yet it is a great moral advance when the guilty have far more to fear from war than the innocent.

In the images of celebrating Iraqis, we have also seen the ageless appeal of human freedom. Decades of lies and intimidation could not make the Iraqi people love their oppressors or desire their own enslavement. Men and women in every culture need liberty like they need food and water and air. Everywhere that freedom arrives, humanity rejoices; and everywhere that freedom stirs, let tyrants fear.

We have difficult work to do in Iraq. We're bringing order to parts of that country that remain dangerous. We're pursuing and finding leaders of the old regime, who will be held to account for their crimes. We've begun the search for hidden chemical and biological weapons and already know of hundreds of sites that will be investigated. We're helping to rebuild Iraq, where the dictator built palaces for himself, instead of hospitals and schools. And we will stand with the new leaders of Iraq as they establish a government of, by, and for the Iraqi people.

The transition from dictatorship to democracy will take time, but it is worth every effort. Our coalition will stay until our work is done. Then we will leave, and we will leave behind a free Iraq.

The battle of Iraq is one victory in a war on terror that began on September the 11, 2001 — and still goes on. That terrible morning, 19 evil men — the shock troops of a hateful ideology — gave America and the civilized world a glimpse of their ambitions. They imagined, in the words of one terrorist, that September the 11th would be the "beginning of the end of America." By seeking to turn our cities into killing fields, terrorists and their allies believed that they could destroy this nation's resolve, and force our retreat from the world. They have failed.

In the battle of Afghanistan, we destroyed the Taliban, many terrorists, and the camps where they trained. We continue to help the Afghan people lay roads, restore hospitals, and educate all of their children. Yet we also have dangerous work to complete. As I speak, a Special Operations task force, led by the 82nd Airborne, is on the trail of the terrorists and those who seek to undermine the free government of Afghanistan. America and our coalition will finish what we have begun.

From Pakistan to the Philippines to the Horn of Africa, we are hunting down al Qaeda killers. Nineteen months ago, I pledged that the terrorists would not escape the patient justice of the United States. And as of tonight, nearly one-half of al Qaeda's senior operatives have been captured or killed.

The liberation of Iraq is a crucial advance in the campaign against terror. We've removed an ally of al Qaeda, and cut off a source of terrorist funding. And this much is certain: No terrorist network will gain weapons of mass destruction from the Iraqi regime, because the regime is no more.

In these 19 months that changed the world, our actions have been focused and deliberate and proportionate to the offense. We have not forgotten the victims of September the 11th — the last phone calls, the cold murder of children, the searches in the rubble. With those attacks, the terrorists and their supporters declared war on the United States. And war is what they got.

Our war against terror is proceeding according to principles that I have made clear to all: Any person involved in committing or planning terrorist attacks against the American people becomes an enemy of this country, and a target of American justice.

Any person, organization, or government that supports, protects, or harbors terrorists is complicit in the murder of the innocent, and equally guilty of terrorist crimes.

Any outlaw regime that has ties to terrorist groups and seeks or possesses weapons of mass destruction is a grave danger to the civilized world — and will be confronted.

And anyone in the world, including the Arab world, who works and sacrifices for freedom has a loyal friend in the United States of America.

Our commitment to liberty is America's tradition — declared at our founding; affirmed in Franklin Roosevelt's Four Freedoms; asserted in the Truman Doctrine and in Ronald Reagan's challenge to an evil empire. We are committed to freedom in Afghanistan, in Iraq, and in a peaceful Palestine. The advance of freedom is the surest strategy to undermine the appeal of terror in the world. Where freedom takes hold, hatred gives way to hope. When freedom takes hold, men and women turn to the peaceful pursuit of a better life. American values and American interests lead in the same direction: We stand for human liberty.

The United States upholds these principles of security and freedom in many ways — with all the tools of diplomacy, law enforcement, intelligence, and finance. We're working with a broad coalition of nations that understand the threat and our shared responsibility to meet it. The use of force has been — and remains — our last resort. Yet all can know, friend and foe alike, that our nation has a mission: We will answer threats to our security, and we will defend the peace.

Our mission continues. Al Qaeda is wounded, not destroyed. The scattered cells of the terrorist network still operate in many nations, and we know from daily intelligence that they continue to plot against free people. The proliferation of deadly weapons remains a serious danger. The enemies of freedom are not idle, and neither are we. Our government has taken unprecedented measures to defend the homeland. And we will continue to hunt down the enemy before he can strike.

The war on terror is not over; yet it is not endless. We do not know the day of final victory, but we have seen the turning of the tide. No act of the terrorists will change our purpose, or weaken our resolve, or alter their fate. Their cause is lost. Free nations will press on to victory.

Other nations in history have fought in foreign lands and remained to occupy and exploit. Americans, following a battle, want nothing more than to return home. And that is your direction tonight. After service in the Afghan — and Iraqi theaters of war — after 100,000 miles, on the longest carrier deployment in recent history, you are homeward bound. Some of you will see new family members for the first time — 150 babies were born while their fathers were on the Lincoln. Your families are proud of you, and your nation will welcome you.

We are mindful, as well, that some good men and women are not making the journey home. One of those who fell, Corporal Jason Mileo, spoke to his parents five days before his death. Jason's father said, "He called us from the center of Baghdad, not to brag, but to tell us he loved us. Our son was a soldier."

Every name, every life is a loss to our military, to our nation, and to the loved ones who grieve. There's no home-coming for these families. Yet we pray, in God's time, their reunion will come.

Those we lost were last seen on duty. Their final act on this Earth was to fight a great evil and bring liberty to others. All of you — all in this generation of our military — have taken up the highest calling of history. You're defending your country, and protecting the innocent from harm. And wher-ever you go, you carry a message of hope — a message that is ancient and ever new. In the words of the prophet Isaiah, "To the captives, 'come out,' — and to those in darkness, 'be free.'"

Thank you for serving our country and our cause.

Progress of Democracy in the Middle East

20th Anniversary, Nat'l Endowment for Democracy
November 6, 2003

Thanks for the warm welcome, and thanks for inviting me to join you in this 20th anniversary of the National Endowment for Democracy. The staff and directors of this organization have seen a lot of history over the last two decades, you've been a part of that history. By speaking for and standing for freedom, you've lifted the hopes of people around the world, and you've brought great credit to America.

I appreciate Vin for the short introduction. I'm a man who likes short introductions. And he didn't let me down. But more importantly, I appreciate the invitation. I appreciate the members of Congress who are here, senators from both political parties, members of the House of Representatives from both political parties. I appreciate the ambassadors who are here. I appreciate the guests who have come. I appreciate the bipartisan spirit, the nonpartisan spirit of the National Endowment for Democracy. I'm glad that Republicans and Democrats and independents are working together to advance human liberty.

The roots of our democracy can be traced to England, and to its Parliament — and so can the roots of this organization. In June of 1982, President Ronald Reagan spoke at Westminster Palace and declared, the turning point had arrived in history. He argued that Soviet communism had failed, precisely because it did not respect its own people — their creativity, their genius and their rights.

President Reagan said that the day of Soviet tyranny was passing, that freedom had a momentum which would not be halted. He gave this organization its mandate: to add

87

to the momentum of freedom across the world. Your mandate was important 20 years ago; it is equally important today.

A number of critics were dismissive of that speech by the President. According to one editorial of the time, "It seems hard to be a sophisticated European and also an admirer of Ronald Reagan." Some observers on both sides of the Atlantic pronounced the speech simplistic and naive, and even dangerous. In fact, Ronald Reagan's words were courageous and optimistic and entirely correct.

The great democratic movement President Reagan described was already well underway. In the early 1970s, there were about 40 democracies in the world. By the middle of that decade, Portugal and Spain and Greece held free elections. Soon there were new democracies in Latin America, and free institutions were spreading in Korea, in Taiwan, and in East Asia. This very week in 1989, there were protests in East Berlin and in Leipzig. By the end of that year, every communist dictatorship in Central America* had collapsed. Within another year, the South African government released Nelson Mandela. Four years later, he was elected president of his country — ascending, like Walesa and Havel, from prisoner of state to head of state.

As the 20th century ended, there were around 120 democracies in the world — and I can assure you more are on the way. Ronald Reagan would be pleased, and he would not be surprised.

We've witnessed, in little over a generation, the swiftest advance of freedom in the 2,500 year story of democracy. Historians in the future will offer their own explanations for why this happened. Yet we already know some of the reasons they will cite. It is no accident that the rise of so many democracies took place in a time when the world's most influential nation was itself a democracy.

The United States made military and moral commitments in Europe and Asia, which protected free nations from aggression, and created the conditions in which new democracies could flourish. As we provided security for whole nations, we also provided inspiration for oppressed peoples. In prison camps, in banned union meetings, in clandestine churches, men and women knew that the whole world was not sharing their own nightmare. They knew of at least one place — a bright and hopeful land — where freedom was valued and secure. And they prayed that America would not forget them, or forget the mission to promote liberty around the world.

Historians will note that in many nations, the advance of markets and free enterprise helped to create a middle class that was confident enough to demand their own rights. They will point to the role of technology in frustrating censorship and central control — and marvel at the power of instant communications to spread the truth, the news, and courage across borders.

Historians in the future will reflect on an extraordinary, undeniable fact: Over time, free nations grow stronger and dictatorships grow weaker. In the middle of the 20th century, some imagined that the central planning and social regimentation were a shortcut to national strength. In fact, the prosperity, and social vitality and technological progress of a people are directly determined by extent of their liberty. Freedom honors and unleashes human creativity — and creativity determines the strength and wealth of nations. Liberty is both the plan of Heaven for humanity, and the best hope for progress here on Earth.

The progress of liberty is a powerful trend. Yet, we also know that liberty, if not defended, can be lost. The success of freedom is not determined by some dialectic of history. By definition, the success of freedom rests upon the choices and the courage of free peoples, and upon their willingness to sacrifice. In the trenches of World War I, through a two-front war in the 1940s, the difficult battles of Korea and Vietnam, and in missions of rescue and liberation on nearly every continent, Americans have amply displayed our willingness to sacrifice for liberty.

The sacrifices of Americans have not always been recognized or appreciated, yet they have been worthwhile. Because we and our allies were steadfast, Germany and Japan are democratic nations that no longer threaten the world. A global nuclear standoff with the Soviet Union ended peacefully — as did the Soviet Union. The nations of Europe are moving towards unity, not dividing into armed camps and descending into genocide. Every nation has learned, or should have learned, an important lesson: Freedom is worth fighting for, dying for, and standing for — and the advance of freedom leads to peace.

And now we must apply that lesson in our own time. We've reached another great turning point — and the resolve we show will shape the next stage of the world democratic movement.

Our commitment to democracy is tested in countries like Cuba and Burma and North Korea and Zimbabwe — outposts of oppression in our world. The people in these nations live in captivity, and fear and silence. Yet, these regimes cannot hold back freedom forever — and, one day, from prison camps and prison cells, and from exile, the leaders of new democracies will arrive. Communism, and militarism and rule by the capricious and corrupt are the relics of a passing era. And we will stand with these oppressed peoples until the day of their freedom finally arrives.

Our commitment to democracy is tested in China. That nation now has a sliver, a fragment of liberty. Yet, China's people will eventually want their liberty pure and whole. China has discovered that economic freedom leads to national wealth. China's leaders will also discover that freedom is indivisible — that social and religious freedom is also essential to national greatness and national dignity. Eventually, men and women who are allowed to control their own wealth will insist on controlling their own lives and their own country.

Our commitment to democracy is also tested in the Middle East, which is my focus today, and must be a focus of American policy for decades to come. In many nations of the Middle East — countries of great strategic importance — democracy has not yet taken root. And the questions arise: Are the peoples of the Middle East somehow beyond the reach of liberty? Are millions of men and women and children condemned by history or culture to live in despotism? Are they alone never to know freedom, and never even to have a choice in the matter? I, for one, do not believe it. I believe every person has the ability and the right to be free.

Some skeptics of democracy assert that the traditions of Islam are inhospitable to the representative government. This "cultural condescension," as Ronald Reagan termed it, has a long history. After the Japanese surrender in 1945, a so-called Japan expert asserted that democracy in that former empire would "never work." Another observer declared the prospects for democracy in post-Hitler Germany are, and I quote, "most uncertain at best" — he made that claim in 1957. Seventy-four years ago, The Sunday London Times declared nine-tenths of the population of India to be "illiterates not caring a fig for politics." Yet when Indian democracy was imperiled in the 1970s, the Indian people showed their commitment to liberty in a national referendum that saved their form of government.

Time after time, observers have questioned whether this country, or that people, or this group, are "ready" for democracy — as if freedom were a prize you win for meeting our own Western standards of progress. In fact, the daily work of democracy itself is the path of progress. It teaches cooperation, the free exchange of ideas, and the peaceful resolution of differences. As men and women are showing, from Bangladesh to Botswana, to Mongolia, it is the practice of democracy that makes a nation ready for democracy, and every nation can start on this path.

It should be clear to all that Islam — the faith of one-fifth of humanity — is consistent with democratic rule. Democratic progress is found in many predominantly Muslim countries — in Turkey and Indonesia, and Senegal and Albania, Niger and Sierra Leone. Muslim men and women are good citizens of India and South Africa, of the nations of Western Europe, and of the United States of America.

More than half of all the Muslims in the world live in freedom under democratically constituted governments. They succeed in democratic societies, not in spite of their faith, but because of it. A religion that demands individual moral accountability, and encourages the encounter of the individual with God, is fully compatible with the rights and responsibilities of self-government.

Yet there's a great challenge today in the Middle East. In the words of a recent report by Arab scholars, the global wave of democracy has — and I quote — "barely reached the Arab states." They continue: "This freedom deficit undermines human development and is one of the most painful manifestations of lagging political development." The freedom deficit they describe has terrible consequences, of the people of the Middle East and for the world. In many Middle Eastern countries, poverty is deep and it is spreading, women lack rights and are denied schooling. Whole societies remain stagnant while the world moves ahead. These are not the failures of a culture or a religion. These are the failures of political and economic doctrines.

As the colonial era passed away, the Middle East saw the establishment of many military dictatorships. Some rulers adopted the dogmas of socialism, seized total control of political parties and the media and universities. They allied themselves with the Soviet bloc and with international terrorism. Dictators in Iraq and Syria promised the restoration of national honor, a return to ancient glories. They've left instead a legacy of torture, oppression, misery, and ruin.

Other men, and groups of men, have gained influence in the Middle East and beyond through an ideology of theocratic terror. Behind their language of religion is the ambition for absolute political power. Ruling cabals like the Taliban show their version of religious piety in public whippings of women, ruthless suppression of any difference or dissent, and support for terrorists who arm and train to murder the innocent. The Taliban promised religious purity and national pride. Instead, by systematically destroying a proud and working society, they left behind suffering and starvation.

Many Middle Eastern governments now understand that military dictatorship and theocratic rule are a straight, smooth highway to nowhere. But some governments still cling to the old habits of central control. There are governments that still fear and repress independent thought and creativity, and private enterprise — the human qualities that make for a — strong and successful societies. Even when these nations have vast natural resources, they do not respect or develop their greatest resources — the talent and energy of men and women working and living in freedom.

Instead of dwelling on past wrongs and blaming others, governments in the Middle East need to confront real problems, and serve the true interests of their nations. The good and capable people of the Middle East all deserve responsible leadership. For too long, many people in that region have been victims and subjects — they deserve to be active citizens.

Governments across the Middle East and North Africa are beginning to see the need for change. Morocco has a diverse new parliament; King Mohammed has urged it to extend the rights to women. Here is how His Majesty explained his reforms to parliament: "How can society achieve progress while women, who represent half the nation, see their rights violated and suffer as a result of injustice, violence, and marginalization, notwithstanding the dignity and justice granted to them by our glorious religion?" The King of Morocco is correct: The future of Muslim nations will be better for all with the full participation of women.

In Bahrain last year, citizens elected their own parliament for the first time in nearly three decades. Oman has extended the vote to all adult citizens; Qatar has a new constitution; Yemen has a multiparty political system; Kuwait has a directly elected national assembly; and Jordan held historic elections this summer. Recent surveys in Arab nations reveal broad support for political pluralism, the rule of law, and free speech. These are the stirrings of Middle Eastern democracy, and they carry the promise of greater change to come.

As changes come to the Middle Eastern region, those with power should ask themselves: Will they be remembered for resisting reform, or for leading it? In Iran, the demand for democracy is strong and broad, as we saw last month when thousands gathered to welcome home Shirin Ebadi, the winner of the Nobel Peace Prize. The regime in Teheran must heed the democratic demands of the Iranian people, or lose its last claim to legitimacy.

For the Palestinian people, the only path to independence and dignity and progress is the path of democracy. (Applause.) And the Palestinian leaders who block and undermine democratic reform, and feed hatred and encourage violence are not leaders at all. They're the main obstacles to peace, and to the success of the Palestinian people.

The Saudi government is taking first steps toward reform, including a plan for gradual introduction of elections. By giving the Saudi people a greater role in their own society, the Saudi government can demonstrate true leadership in the region.

The great and proud nation of Egypt has shown the way toward peace in the Middle East, and now should show the way toward democracy in the Middle East.

Champions of democracy in the region understand that democracy is not perfect, it is not the path to utopia, but it's the only path to national success and dignity.

As we watch and encourage reforms in the region, we are mindful that modernization is not the same as Westernization. Representative governments in the Middle East will reflect their own cultures. They will not, and should not, look like us. Democratic nations may be constitutional monarchies, federal republics, or parliamentary systems. And working democracies always need time to develop — as did our own. We've taken a 200 year journey toward inclusion and justice — and this makes us patient and understanding as other nations are at different stages of this journey.

There are, however, essential principles common to every successful society, in every culture. Successful societies limit the power of the state and the power of the military — so that governments respond to the will of the people, and not the will of an elite. Successful societies protect freedom with the consistent and impartial rule of law, instead of selecting applying — selectively applying the law to punish political opponents. Successful societies allow room for healthy civic institutions — for political parties and labor unions and independent newspapers and broadcast media. Successful societies guarantee religious liberty — the right to serve and honor God without fear of persecution. Successful societies privatize their economies, and secure the rights of property. They prohibit and punish official corruption, and invest in the health and education of their people. They recognize the rights of women. And instead of directing hatred and resentment against others, successful societies appeal to the hopes of their own people.

These vital principles are being applies in the nations of Afghanistan and Iraq. With the steady leadership of President Karzai, the people of Afghanistan are building a modern and peaceful government. Next month, 500 delegates will convene a national assembly in Kabul to approve a new Afghan constitution. The proposed draft would establish a bicameral parliament, set national elections next year, and recognize Afghanistan's Muslim identity, while protecting the rights of all citizens. Afghanistan faces continuing economic and security challenges — it will face those challenges as a free and stable democracy.

In Iraq, the Coalition Provisional Authority and the Iraqi Governing Council are also working together to build a democracy — and after three decades of tyranny, this work is not easy. The former dictator ruled by terror and treachery, and left deeply ingrained habits of fear and distrust. Remnants of his regime, joined by foreign terrorists, continue their battle against order and against civilization. Our coalition is responding to recent attacks with precision raids, guided by intelligence provided by the Iraqis, themselves. And we're working closely with Iraqi citizens as they prepare a constitution, as they move toward free elections and take increasing responsibility for their own affairs. As in the defense of Greece in 1947, and later in the Berlin Airlift, the strength and will of free peoples are now being tested before a watching world. And we will meet this test.

Securing democracy in Iraq is the work of many hands. American and coalition forces are sacrificing for the peace of Iraq and for the security of free nations. Aid workers from many countries are facing danger to help the Iraqi people. The National Endowment for Democracy is promoting women's rights, and training Iraqi journalists, and teaching the skills of political participation. Iraqis, themselves — police and borders guards and local officials — are joining in the work and they are sharing in the sacrifice.

This is a massive and difficult undertaking — it is worth our effort, it is worth our sacrifice, because we know the stakes. The failure of Iraqi democracy would embolden terrorists around the world, increase dangers to the American people, and extinguish the hopes of millions in the region. Iraqi democracy will succeed — and that success will send forth the news, from Damascus to Teheran — that freedom can be the future of every nation. The establishment of a free Iraq at the heart of the Middle East will be a watershed event in the global democratic revolution.

Sixty years of Western nations excusing and accommodating the lack of freedom in the Middle East did nothing to make us safe — because in the long run, stability cannot be purchased at the expense of liberty. As long as the Middle East remains a place where freedom does not flourish, it will remain a place of stagnation, resentment, and violence ready for export. And with the spread of weapons that can bring catastrophic harm to our country and to our friends, it would be reckless to accept the status quo.

Therefore, the United States has adopted a new policy, a forward strategy of freedom in the Middle East. This strategy requires the same persistence and energy and idealism we have shown before. And it will yield the same results. As in Europe, as in Asia, as in every region of the world, the advance of freedom leads to peace.

The advance of freedom is the calling of our time; it is the calling of our country. From the Fourteen Points to the Four Freedoms, to the Speech at Westminster, America has put our power at the service of principle. We believe that liberty is the design of nature; we believe that liberty is the direction of history. We believe that human fulfillment and excellence come in the responsible exercise of liberty. And we believe that freedom — the freedom we prize — is not for us alone, it is the right and the capacity of all mankind.

Working for the spread of freedom can be hard. Yet,

America has accomplished hard tasks before. Our nation is strong; we're strong of heart. And we're not alone. Freedom is finding allies in every country; freedom finds allies in every culture. And as we meet the terror and violence of the world, we can be certain the author of freedom is not indifferent to the fate of freedom.

With all the tests and all the challenges of our age, this is, above all, the age of liberty. Each of you at this Endowment is fully engaged in the great cause of liberty. And I thank you.

WE DID NOT CHARGE ONLY TO RETREAT

WHITEHALL PALACE, BRITAIN
NOVEMBER 19, 2003

It was pointed out to me that the last noted American to visit London stayed in a glass box dangling over the Thames.

A few might have been happy to provide similar arrangements for me.

I thank Her Majesty, the queen, for interceding. We're honored to be staying at her house.

Americans traveling to England always observe more similarities to our country than differences. I've been here only a short time, but I've noticed the tradition of free speech exercised with enthusiasm is alive and well here in London.

We have that at home too. They now have that right in Baghdad as well.

The people of Great Britain also might see some familiar traits in Americans.

We're sometimes faulted for a naive faith that liberty can change the world. If that's an error, it began with reading too much John Locke and Adam Smith.

Americans have on occasion been called moralists, who often speak in terms of right and wrong. That zeal has been inspired by examples on this island, by the tireless compassion of Lord Shaftesbury, the righteous courage of Wilberforce and the firm determination of the Royal Navy over the decades to fight and end the trade in slaves.

It's rightly said that Americans are a religious people. That's in part because of the good news that was translated by Tyndale, preached by Wesley, lived out in the example of William Booth.

99

At times Americans are even said to have a puritan streak. And where might that have come from? Well, we can start with the Puritans.

To this fine heritage, Americans have added a few traits of our own: the good influence of our immigrants and the spirit of the frontier.

Yet there remains a bit of England in every American. So much of our national character comes from you, and we're glad for it. The fellowship of generations is the cause of common beliefs.

We believe in open societies ordered by moral conviction. We believe in private markets humanized by compassionate government. We believe in economies that reward effort, communities that protect the weak and the duty of nations to respect the dignity and the rights of all. And whether one learns these ideals in County Durham or in West Texas, they instill mutual respect and they inspire common purpose.

More than an alliance of security and commerce, the British and American peoples have an alliance of values. And today this old and tested alliance is very strong.

The deepest beliefs of our nations set the direction of our foreign policy. We value our own civil rights, so we stand for the human rights of others. We affirm the God-given dignity of every person, so we are moved to action by poverty and oppression and famine and disease.

The United States and Great Britain share a mission in the world beyond the balance of power or the simple pursuit of interest.

We seek the advance of freedom and the peace that freedom brings.

Together our nations are standing and sacrificing for this high goal in a distant land at this very hour. And America honors the idealism and the bravery of the sons and daughters of Britain.

The last president to stay at Buckingham Palace was an idealist without question. At a dinner hosted by King George V in 1918, Woodrow Wilson made a pledge. With typical American understatement, he vowed that right and justice would become the predominant and controlling force in the world.

President Wilson had come to Europe with his 14 points for peace. Many complementing him on this vision yet some were dubious.

Take, for example, the prime minister of France. He complained that God himself had only 10 commandments.

Sounds familiar.

At Wilson's high point of idealism, however, Europe was one short generation from Munich and Auschwitz and the Blitz.

Looking back, we see the reasons why. The League of Nations, lacking both credibility and will, collapsed at the first challenge of the dictators.

Free nations failed to recognize, much less confront, the aggressive evil in plain sight. And so, dictators went about their business, feeding resentments and anti-Semitism, bringing death to innocent people in this city and across the world and filling the last century with violence and genocide.

Through world war and cold war we learned that idealism, if it is to do any good in this world, requires common purpose and national strength, moral courage and patience in difficult tasks. And now our generation has need of these qualities.

On September the 11th, 2001, the terrorists left their mark of murder on my country and took the lives of 67 British citizens. With the passing of months and years, it is the natural human desire to resume a quiet life and to put that day behind us as if waking from a dark dream. The hope that danger has passed is comforting, is understanding and it is false.

The attacks that followed in Bali, Jakarta, Casablanca, Bombay, Mombasa, Najaf, Jerusalem, Riyadh, Baghdad and Istanbul were not dreams. They're part of a global campaign by terrorist networks to intimidate and demoralize all who oppose them.

These terrorists target the innocent and they kill by the thousands. And they would, if they gain the weapons they seek, kill by the millions and not be finished.

The greatest threat of our age is nuclear, chemical or biological weapons in the hands of terrorists and the dictators who aid them.

The evil is in plain sight. The danger only increases with denial. Great responsibilities fall once again to the great democracies. We will face these threats with open eyes and we will defeat them.

The peace and security of free nations now rests on three pillars.

First, international organizations must be equal to the challenges facing our world, from lifting up failing states to opposing proliferation. Like 11 presidents before me, I believe in the international institutions and alliances that America helped to form and helps to lead.

The United States and Great Britain have labored hard to help make the United Nations what it is supposed to be: an effective instrument of our collective security.

In recent months, we've sought and gained three additional resolutions on Iraq, Resolutions 1441, 1483 and 1511, precisely because the global danger of terror demands a global response.

The United Nations has no more compelling advocate than your prime minister, who at every turn has championed its ideals and appealed to its authority. He understands as well that the credibility of the U.N. depends on a willingness to keep its word and to act when action is required.

America and Great Britain have done, and will do, all in

their power to prevent the United Nations from solemnly choosing its own irrelevance and inviting the fate of the League of Nations.

It's not enough to meet the dangers of the world with resolutions; we must meet those dangers with resolve.

In this century, as in the last, nations can accomplish more together than apart. For 54 years America has stood with our partners in NATO, the most effective multilateral institution in history.

We're committed to this great democratic alliance and we believe it must have the will and the capacity to act beyond Europe where threats emerge.

My nation welcomes the growing unity of Europe, and the world needs America and the European Union to work in common purpose for the advance of security and justice.

America is cooperating with four other nations to meet the dangers posed by North Korea. America believes the IAEA must be true to its purpose and hold Iran to its obligations. Our first choice and our constant practice is to work with other responsible governments.

We understand as well that the success of multilateralism is not measured by adherence to forms alone — the tidiness of the process — but by the results we achieve to keep our nations secure.

The second pillar of peace and security in our world is the willingness of free nations, when the last resort arrives, to retain aggression and evil by force.

There are principled objections to the use of force in every generation, and I credit the good motives behind these views.

Those in authority, however, are not judged only by good motivations. The people have given us the duty to defend them and that duty sometimes requires the violent restraint of violent men. In some cases, the measured use of force is all that protects us from a chaotic world ruled by force.

Most in the peaceful West have no living memory of that kind of world. Yet in some countries the memories are recent.

The victims of ethnic cleansing in the Balkans, those who survived the rapists and the death squads had few qualms when NATO applied force to help end those crimes. The women of Afghanistan, imprisoned in their homes and beaten in the streets and executed in public spectacles, did not reproach us for routing the Taliban.

Inhabitants of Iraq's Baathist hell, with his lavish palaces and his torture chambers, with his massive statutes and its mass graves, do not miss their fugitive dictator; they rejoiced at his fall.

In all these cases, military action was preceded by diplomatic initiatives and negotiations and ultimatums and final chances until the final moment.

In Iraq, year after year, the dictator was given the chance to account for his weapons programs and end the nightmare for his people. Now the resolutions he defied have been enforced.

And who will say that Iraq was better off when Saddam Hussein was strutting and killing, or that the world was safer when he held power?

Who doubts that Afghanistan is a more just society and less dangerous without Mullah Omar playing host to terrorists from around the world?

And Europe, too, is plainly better off with Milosevic answering for his crimes instead of committing more.

It's been said that those who live near a police station find it hard to believe in the triumph of violence. In the same way, free peoples might be tempted to take for granted the orderly societies we have come to know.

Europe's peaceful unity is one of the great achievements of the last half century. And because European countries now resolve differences through negotiation and consensus, there's sometimes an assumption that the entire world functions in the same way.

But let us never forget how Europe's unity was achieved: by Allied armies of liberation and NATO armies of defense.

And let us never forget, beyond Europe's borders, in a world where oppression and violence are very real, liberation is still a moral goal and freedom and security still need defenders.

The third pillar of security is our commitment to the global expansion of democracy and the hope and progress it brings as the alternative to instability and hatred and terror. We cannot rely exclusively on military power to assure our long-term security. Lasting peace is gained as justice and democracy advance.

In democratic and successful societies, men and women do not swear allegiance to malcontents and murderers. They turn their hearts and labor to building better lives. And democratic governments do not shelter terrorist camps or attack their peaceful neighbors.

They honor the aspirations and dignity of their own people.

In our conflict with terror and tyranny, we have an unmatched advantage, a power that cannot be resisted, and that is the appeal of freedom to all mankind.

As global powers, both our nations serve the cause of freedom in many ways in many places.

By promoting development and fighting famine and AIDS and other diseases, we're fulfilling our moral duties as well as encouraging stability and building a firmer basis for democratic institutions.

By working for justice in Burma, the Sudan and in Zimbabwe, we give hope to suffering people and improve the chances for stability and progress.

By extending the reach of trade, we foster prosperity and the habits of liberty.

And by advancing freedom in the greater Middle East, we help end a cycle of dictatorship and radicalism that brings millions of people to misery and brings danger to our own people.

The stakes in that region could not be higher.

If the Middle East remains a place where freedom does not flourish, it will remain a place of stagnation and anger and violence for export. And as we saw in the ruins of two towers, no distance on the map will protect our lives and way of life.

If the greater Middle East joins the democratic revolution that has reached much of the world, the lives of millions in that region will be bettered, and a trend of conflict and fear will be ended at its source.

The movement of history will not come about quickly. Because of our own democratic development, the fact that it was gradual and at times turbulent, we must be patient with others.

And the Middle East countries have some distance to travel. Arab scholars speak of a freedom deficit that has separated whole nations from the progress of our time. The essentials of social and material progress — limited government, equal justice under law, religious and economic liberty, political participation, free press and respect for the rights of women — have been scarce across the region. Yet that has begun to change.

In an arc of reform from Morocco to Jordan to Qatar, we are seeing elections and new protections for women and the stirrings of political pluralism.

Many governments are realizing that theocracy and dictatorship do not lead to national greatness; they end in national ruin. They're finding, as others will find, that national progress and dignity are achieved when governments are just and people are free.

The democratic progress we've seen in the Middle East

was not imposed from abroad, and neither will the greater progress we hope to see. Freedom, by definition, must be chosen and defended by those who choose it.

Our part as free nations is to ally ourselves with reform wherever it occurs.

Perhaps the most helpful change we can make is to change in our own thinking. In the West, there's been a certain skepticism about the capacity or even the desire of Middle Eastern peoples for self- government.

We're told that Islam is somehow inconsistent with a democratic culture, yet more than half of the world's Muslims are today contributing citizens in democratic societies.

It is suggested that the poor, in their daily struggles, care little for self-government, yet the poor especially need the power of democracy to defend themselves against corrupt elites.

People from the Middle East share a high civilization, a religion of personal responsibility and a need for freedom as deep as our own.

It is not realism to suppose that one-fifth of humanity is unsuited to liberty. It is pessimism and condescension, and we should have none of it.

We must shake off decades of failed policy in the Middle East. Your nation and mine in the past have been willing to make a bargain to tolerate oppression for the sake of stability. Longstanding ties often led us to overlook the faults of local elites.

Yet this bargain did not bring stability or make us safe. It merely bought time while problems festered and ideologies of violence took hold.

As recent history has shown, we cannot turn a blind eye to oppression just because the oppression is not in our own back yard. No longer should we think tyranny is benign because it is temporarily convenient. Tyranny is never benign to its victims and our great democracies should oppose tyranny wherever it is found.

Now we're pursuing a different course, a forward strategy of freedom in the Middle East. We will consistently challenge the enemies of reform and confront the allies of terror. We will expect a higher standard from our friends in the region, and we will meet our responsibilities in Afghanistan and in Iraq by finishing the work of democracy we have begun.

There were good-faith disagreements in your country and mine over the course and timing of military action in Iraq. Whatever has come before, we now have only two options: to keep our word or to break our word.

The failure of democracy in Iraq would throw its people back into misery and turn that country over to terrorists who wish to destroy us. Yet democracy will succeed in Iraq, because our will is firm, our word is good and the Iraqi people will not surrender their freedom.

Since the liberation of Iraq, we have seen changes that could hardly have been imagined a year ago. A new Iraqi police force protects the people, instead of bullying them. More than 150 Iraqi newspapers are now in circulation, printing what they choose, not what they're ordered.

Schools are open, with textbooks free of propaganda. Hospitals are functioning and are well-supplied.

Iraq has a new currency, the first battalion of a new army, representative local governments, and a governing council with an aggressive timetable for national sovereignty.

This is substantial progress. And much of it has proceeded faster than similar efforts in Germany and Japan after World War II.

But the violence we are seeing in Iraq today is serious. And it comes from Baathist holdouts and jihadists from other countries and terrorists drawn to the prospect of innocent bloodshed.

It is the nature of terrorism and the cruelty of a few to

try to bring grief and the loss to many.

The armed forces of both our countries have taken losses felt deeply by our citizens. Some families now live with the burden of great sorrow.

Cannot take the pain away, but these families can know they are not alone. We pray for their strength. We pray for their comfort. And we will never forget the courage of the ones they loved.

The terrorists have a purpose, a strategy to their cruelty. They view the rise of democracy in Iraq as a powerful threat to their ambitions. In this, they are correct.

They believe their acts of terror against our coalition, against international aid workers and against innocent Iraqis will make us recoil and retreat. In this, they are mistaken.

We did not charge hundreds of miles into the heart of Iraq and pay a bitter cost of casualties and liberate 25 million people only to retreat before a band of thugs and assassins.

We will help the Iraqi people establish a peaceful and democratic country in the heart of the Middle East. And by doing so, we will defend our people from danger.

A forward strategy of freedom must also apply to the Arab-Israeli conflict. This is a difficult period in a part of the world that has known many. Yet our commitment remains firm. We seek justice and dignity. We seek a viable, independent state for the Palestinian people, who have been betrayed by others for too long.

We seek security and recognition for the state of Israel, which has lived in the shadow of random death for too long.

These are worthy goals in themselves. And by reaching them, we will also remove an occasion and excuse for hatred and violence in the broader Middle East.

Achieving peace in the Holy Land is not just a matter of the shape of a border. As we work on the details of peace, we must look to the heart of the matter, which is the need for a viable Palestinian democracy.

Peace will not be achieved by Palestinian rulers who intimidate opposition, who tolerate and profit from corruption and maintain their ties to terrorist groups. These are the methods of the old elites, who time and again have put their own self-interest above the interests of the people they claim to serve.

The long-suffering Palestinian people deserve better. They deserve true leaders, capable of creating and governing a Palestinian state.

Even after the setbacks and frustrations of recent months, goodwill and hard effort can bring about a Palestinian state and a secure Israel.

Those who would lead a new Palestine should adopt peaceful means to achieve the rights of their people and create the reformed institutions of a stable democracy.

Israel should free settlement construction, dismantle unauthorized outposts, end the daily humiliation of the Palestinian people and not prejudice final negotiations with the placements of walls and fences.

Arab states should end incitement in their own media, cut off public and private funding for terrorism, and establish normal relations with Israel.

Leaders in Europe should withdraw all favor and support from any Palestinian ruler who fails his people and betrays their cause.

And Europe's leaders, and all leaders, should strongly oppose anti-Semitism, which poisons public debates over the future of the Middle East.

Ladies and gentlemen, we have great objectives before us that make our Atlantic alliance as vital as it has ever been.

We will encourage the strength and effectiveness of international institutions. We will use force when necessary in the defense of freedom.

And we will raise up an ideal of democracy in every

part of the world.

On these three pillars we will build the peace and security of all free nations in a time of danger.

So much good has come from our alliance of conviction and might. So much now depends on the strength of this alliance as we go forward.

America has always found strong partners in London, leaders of good judgment and blunt counsel and backbone, when times are tough. And I found all those qualities in your current prime minister, who has my respect and my deepest thanks.

The ties between our nations, however, are deeper than a relationship between leaders. These ties endure because they are formed by the experience and responsibilities and adversity we have shared.

And in the memory of our peoples, there will always be one experience, one central event, when the seal was fixed on the friendship between Britain and the United States: The arrival in

Great Britain of more than 1.5 million American soldiers and airmen in the 1940s was a turning point in the Second World War.

For many Britons, it was a first close look at Americans other than in the movies. Some of you here today may still remember the friendly invasion. Our lads, they took some getting used to.

There was even a saying about what many of them were up to in addition to being overpaid and over here.

At a reunion in North London some years ago, an American pilot who had settled in England after his military service said, "Well, I'm still over here and probably overpaid, so two out of three isn't bad."

In that time of war, the English people did get used to the Americans. They welcomed soldiers and flyers into their villages and homes and took to calling them "our boys."

About 70,000 of those boys did their part to affirm our special relationship. They returned home with English brides.

Americans were getting a certain image of Britain as well. We saw an island threatened on every side with a leader who did not waiver in a country of the firmest character.

And that has not changed. The British people are the sort of partners you want when serious work needs doing. The men and women of this kingdom are kind and steadfast and generous and brave, and America is fortunate to call this country our closest friend in the world. May God bless you all.

Saddam Hussein Captured
The White House Cabinet Room
December 14, 2003

Yesterday, December the 13th, at around 8:30 p.m. Baghdad time, United States military forces captured Saddam Hussein alive. He was found near a farmhouse outside the city of Tikrit, in a swift raid conducted without casualties. And now the former dictator of Iraq will face the justice he denied to millions.

The capture of this man was crucial to the rise of a free Iraq. It marks the end of the road for him, and for all who bullied and killed in his name. For the Baathist holdouts largely responsible for the current violence, there will be no return to the corrupt power and privilege they once held. For the vast majority of Iraqi citizens who wish to live as free men and women, this event brings further assurance that the torture chambers and the secret police are gone forever.

And this afternoon, I have a message for the Iraqi people: You will not have to fear the rule of Saddam Hussein ever again. All Iraqis who take the side of freedom have taken the winning side. The goals of our coalition are the same as your goals — sovereignty for your country, dignity for your great culture, and for every Iraqi citizen, the opportunity for a better life.

In the history of Iraq, a dark and painful era is over. A hopeful day has arrived. All Iraqis can now come together and reject violence and build a new Iraq.

The success of yesterday's mission is a tribute to our men and women now serving in Iraq. The operation was based on the superb work of intelligence analysts who found the dictator's footprints in a vast country. The operation was carried out with skill and precision by a brave fighting force. Our servicemen and women and our coalition allies have faced many dangers in the hunt for members of the fallen regime, and in their effort to bring hope and freedom to the Iraqi people. Their work continues, and so do the risks. Today, on behalf of the nation, I thank the members of our Armed Forces and I congratulate them.

I also have a message for all Americans: The capture of Saddam Hussein does not mean the end of violence in Iraq. We still face terrorists who would rather go on killing the innocent than accept the rise of liberty in the heart of the Middle East. Such men are a direct threat to the American people, and they will be defeated.

We've come to this moment through patience and resolve and focused action. And that is our strategy moving forward. The war on terror is a different kind of war, waged capture by capture, cell by cell, and victory by victory. Our security is assured by our perseverance and by our sure belief in the success of liberty. And the United States of America will not relent until this war is won.

May God bless the people of Iraq, and may God bless America.

2004 STATE OF THE UNION

As we gather tonight, hundreds of thousands of American servicemen and women are deployed across the world in the war on terror. By bringing hope to the oppressed, and delivering justice to the violent, they are making America more secure.

Each day, law enforcement personnel and intelligence officers are tracking terrorist threats; analysts are examining airline passenger lists; the men and women of our new Homeland Security Department are patrolling our coasts and borders.

And their vigilance is protecting America. Americans are proving once again to be the hardest working people in the world. The American economy is growing stronger. The tax relief you passed is working.

Tonight, members of Congress can take pride in the great works of compassion and reform that skeptics had thought impossible. You're raising the standards for our public schools, and you are giving our senior citizens prescription drug coverage under Medicare.

We have faced serious challenges together, and now we face a choice: We can go forward with confidence and resolve, or we can turn back to the dangerous illusion that terrorists are not plotting and outlaw regimes are no threat to us. We can press on with economic growth, and reforms in education and Medicare, or we can turn back to old policies and old divisions.

We've not come all this way — through tragedy, and trial and war — only to falter and leave our work unfinished. Americans are rising to the tasks of history, and they expect the same from us. In their efforts, their enterprise, and their character, the American people are showing that the state of our union is confident and strong.

Our greatest responsibility is the active defense of the American people. Twenty-eight months have passed since September 11th, 2001 — over two years without an attack on American soil. And it is tempting to believe that the danger is behind us. That hope is understandable, comforting — and false. The killing has continued in Bali, Jakarta, Casablanca, Riyadh, Mombasa, Jerusalem, Istanbul, and Baghdad. The terrorists continue to plot against America and the civilized world. And by our will and courage, this danger will be defeated.

Inside the United States, where the war began, we must continue to give our homeland security and law enforcement personnel every tool they need to defend us. And one of those essential tools is the Patriot Act, which allows federal law enforcement to better share information, to track terrorists, to disrupt their cells, and to seize their assets. For years, we have used similar provisions to catch embezzlers and drug traffickers. If these methods are good for hunting criminals, they are even more important for hunting terrorists.

Key provisions of the Patriot Act are set to expire next year. The terrorist threat will not expire on that schedule. Our law enforcement needs this vital legislation to protect our citizens. You need to renew the Patriot Act.

America is on the offensive against the terrorists who started this war. Last March, Khalid Shaikh Mohammed, a mastermind of September the 11th, awoke to find himself in the custody of U.S. and Pakistani authorities. Last August the 11th brought the capture of the terrorist Hambali, who was a key player in the attack in Indonesia that killed over 200 people. We're tracking al Qaeda around the world, and nearly two-thirds of their known leaders have now been captured or killed. Thousands of very skilled and determined military personnel are on the manhunt, going after the remaining killers who hide in cities and caves, and one by one, we will bring these terrorists to justice.

As part of the offensive against terror, we are also confronting the regimes that harbor and support terrorists, and could supply them with nuclear, chemical or biological weapons. The United States and our allies are determined: We refuse to live in the shadow of this ultimate danger.

The first to see our determination were the Taliban, who made Afghanistan the primary training base of al Qaeda killers. As of this month, that country has a new constitution, guaranteeing free elections and full participation by women. Businesses are opening, health care centers are being established, and the boys and girls of Afghanistan are back in school. With the help from the new Afghan army, our coalition is leading aggressive raids against the surviving members of the Taliban and al Qaeda. The men and women of Afghanistan are building a nation that is free and proud and fighting terror — and America is honored to be their friend.

Since we last met in this chamber, combat forces of the United States, Great Britain, Australia, Poland and other countries enforced the demands of the United Nations, ended the rule of Saddam Hussein, and the people of Iraq are free.

Having broken the Baathist regime, we face a remnant of violent Saddam supporters. Men who ran away from our troops in battle are now dispersed and attack from the shadows. These killers, joined by foreign terrorists, are a serious, continuing danger. Yet we're making progress against them. The once all-powerful ruler of Iraq was found in a hole, and now sits in a prison cell. Of the top 55 officials of the former regime, we have captured or killed 45. Our forces are on the offensive, leading over 1,600 patrols a day and conducting an average of 180 raids a week. We are dealing with these thugs in Iraq, just as surely as we dealt with Saddam Hussein's evil regime.

The work of building a new Iraq is hard, and it is right.

And America has always been willing to do what it takes for what is right. Last January, Iraq's only law was the whim of one brutal man. Today our coalition is working with the Iraqi Governing Council to draft a basic law, with a bill of rights. We're working with Iraqis and the United Nations to prepare for a transition to full Iraqi sovereignty by the end of June.

As democracy takes hold in Iraq, the enemies of freedom will do all in their power to spread violence and fear. They are trying to shake the will of our country and our friends, but the United States of America will never be intimidated by thugs and assassins. The killers will fail, and the Iraqi people will live in freedom.

Month by month, Iraqis are assuming more responsibility for their own security and their own future. And tonight we are honored to welcome one of Iraq's most respected leaders: the current President of the Iraqi Governing Council, Adnan Pachachi.

Sir, America stands with you and the Iraqi people as you build a free and peaceful nation.

Because of American leadership and resolve, the world is changing for the better. Last month, the leader of Libya voluntarily pledged to disclose and dismantle all of his regime's weapons of mass destruction programs, including a uranium enrichment project for nuclear weapons. Colonel Qadhafi correctly judged that his country would be better off and far more secure without weapons of mass murder.

Nine months of intense negotiations involving the United States and Great Britain succeeded with Libya, while 12 years of diplomacy with Iraq did not. And one reason is clear: For diplomacy to be effective, words must be credible, and no one can now doubt the word of America.

Different threats require different strategies. Along with nations in the region, we're insisting that North Korea eliminate its nuclear program. America and the international community are demanding that Iran meet its commitments and not develop nuclear weapons. America is committed to keeping the world's most dangerous weapons out of the hands of the most dangerous regimes.

When I came to this rostrum on September the 20th, 2001, I brought the police shield of a fallen officer, my reminder of lives that ended, and a task that does not end. I gave to you and to all Americans my complete commitment to securing our country and defeating our enemies. And this pledge, given by one, has been kept by many.

You in the Congress have provided the resources for our defense, and cast the difficult votes of war and peace. Our closest allies have been unwavering. America's intelligence personnel and diplomats have been skilled and tireless. And the men and women of the American military — they have taken the hardest duty. We've seen their skill and their courage in armored charges and midnight raids, and lonely hours on faithful watch. We have seen the joy when they return, and felt the sorrow when one is lost. I've had the honor of meeting our servicemen and women at many posts, from the deck of a carrier in the Pacific to a mess hall in Baghdad.

Many of our troops are listening tonight. And I want you and your families to know: America is proud of you. And my administration, and this Congress, will give you the resources you need to fight and win the war on terror.

I know that some people question if America is really in a war at all. They view terrorism more as a crime, a problem to be solved mainly with law enforcement and indictments. After the World Trade Center was first attacked in 1993, some of the guilty were indicted and tried and convicted, and sent to prison. But the matter was not settled. The terrorists were still training and plotting in other nations, and drawing up more ambitious plans. After the chaos and carnage of September the 11th, it is not enough to serve our enemies with legal papers. The terrorists and their supporters declared war on the United States, and war is what they got.

Some in this chamber, and in our country, did not support the liberation of Iraq. Objections to war often come from principled motives. But let us be candid about the consequences of leaving Saddam Hussein in power. We're seeking all the facts. Already, the Kay Report identified dozens of weapons of mass destruction-related program activities and significant amounts of equipment that Iraq concealed from the United Nations. Had we failed to act, the dictator's weapons of mass destruction programs would continue to this day. Had we failed to act, Security Council resolutions on Iraq would have been revealed as empty threats, weakening the United Nations and encouraging defiance by dictators around the world. Iraq's torture chambers would still be filled with victims, terrified and innocent. The killing fields of Iraq — where hundreds of thousands of men and women and children vanished into the sands — would still be known only to the killers. For all who love freedom and peace, the world without Saddam Hussein's regime is a better and safer place.

Some critics have said our duties in Iraq must be internationalized. This particular criticism is hard to explain to our partners in Britain, Australia, Japan, South Korea, the Philippines, Thailand, Italy, Spain, Poland, Denmark, Hungary, Bulgaria, Ukraine, Romania, the Netherlands — Norway, El Salvador, and the 17 other countries that have committed troops to Iraq. As we debate at home, we must never ignore the vital contributions of our international partners, or dismiss their sacrifices.

From the beginning, America has sought international support for our operations in Afghanistan and Iraq, and we have gained much support. There is a difference, however, between leading a coalition of many nations, and submitting to the objections of a few. America will never seek a permission slip to defend the security of our country.

We also hear doubts that democracy is a realistic goal for the greater Middle East, where freedom is rare. Yet it is mistaken, and condescending, to assume that whole cultures and great religions are incompatible with liberty and self-government. I believe that God has planted in every human heart the desire to live in freedom. And even when that desire is crushed by tyranny for decades, it will rise again.

As long as the Middle East remains a place of tyranny and despair and anger, it will continue to produce men and movements that threaten the safety of America and our friends. So America is pursuing a forward strategy of freedom in the greater Middle East. We will challenge the enemies of reform, confront the allies of terror, and expect a higher standard from our friend. To cut through the barriers of hateful propaganda, the Voice of America and other broadcast services are expanding their programming in Arabic and Persian — and soon, a new television service will begin providing reliable news and information across the region. I will send you a proposal to double the budget of the National Endowment for Democracy, and to focus its new work on the development of free elections, and free markets, free press, and free labor unions in the Middle East. And above all, we will finish the historic work of democracy in Afghanistan and Iraq, so those nations can light the way for others, and help transform a troubled part of the world.

America is a nation with a mission, and that mission comes from our most basic beliefs. We have no desire to dominate, no ambitions of empire. Our aim is a democratic peace — a peace founded upon the dignity and rights of every man and woman. America acts in this cause with friends and allies at our side, yet we understand our special calling: This great republic will lead the cause of freedom.

In the last three years, adversity has also revealed the fundamental strengths of the American economy. We have come through recession, and terrorist attack, and corporate scandals, and the uncertainties of war. And because you acted to stimulate our economy with tax relief, this economy is strong, and growing stronger.

You have doubled the child tax credit from $500 to $1,000, reduced the marriage penalty, begun to phase out the death tax, reduced taxes on capital gains and stock dividends, cut taxes on small businesses, and you have lowered taxes for every American who pays income taxes.

Americans took those dollars and put them to work, driving this economy forward. The pace of economic growth in the third quarter of 2003 was the fastest in nearly 20 years; new home construction, the highest in almost 20 years; home ownership rates, the highest ever. Manufacturing activity is increasing. Inflation is low. Interest rates are low. Exports are growing. Productivity is high, and jobs are on the rise.

These numbers confirm that the American people are using their money far better than government would have — and you were right to return it.

America's growing economy is also a changing economy. As technology transforms the way almost every job is done, America becomes more productive, and workers need new skills. Much of our job growth will be found in high-skilled fields like health care and biotechnology. So we must respond by helping more Americans gain the skills to find good jobs in our new economy.

All skills begin with the basics of reading and math, which are supposed to be learned in the early grades of our schools. Yet for too long, for too many children, those skills were never mastered. By passing the No Child Left Behind Act, you have made the expectation of literacy the law of our country. We're providing more funding for our schools — a 36-percent increase since 2001. We're requiring higher standards. We are regularly testing every child on the fundamentals. We are reporting results to parents, and making sure they have better options when schools are not performing.

We are making progress toward excellence for every child in America.

But the status quo always has defenders. Some want to undermine the No Child Left Behind Act by weakening standards and accountability. Yet the results we require are really a matter of common sense: We expect third graders to read and do math at the third grade level — and that's not asking too much. Testing is the only way to identify and help students who are falling behind. This nation will not go back to the days of simply shuffling children along from grade to grade without them learning the basics. I refuse to give up on any child — and the No Child Left Behind Act is opening the door of opportunity to all of America's children.

At the same time, we must ensure that older students and adults can gain the skills they need to find work now. Many of the fastest growing occupations require strong math and science preparation, and training beyond the high school level. So tonight, I propose a series of measures called Jobs for the 21st Century. This program will provide extra help to middle and high school students who fall behind in reading and math, expand advanced placement programs in low-income schools, invite math and science professionals from the private sector to teach part-time in our high schools. I propose larger Pell grants for students who prepare for college with demanding courses in high school. I propose increasing our support for America's fine community colleges, so they can — I do so, so they can train workers for industries that are creating the most new jobs. By all these actions, we'll help more and more Americans to join in the growing prosperity of our country. Job training is important, and so is job creation.

We must continue to pursue an aggressive, pro-growth economic agenda. Congress has some unfinished business on the issue of taxes. The tax reductions you passed are set to expire. Unless you act — unless you act — unless you act, the unfair tax on marriage will go back up. Unless you act, millions of families will be charged $300 more in federal taxes for every child. Unless you act, small businesses will pay higher taxes. Unless you act, the death tax will eventually come back to life. Unless you act, Americans face a tax increase. What Congress has given, the Congress should not take away. For the sake of job growth, the tax cuts you passed should be permanent.

Our agenda for jobs and growth must help small business owners and employees with relief from needless federal regulation, and protect them from junk and frivolous lawsuits.

Consumers and businesses need reliable supplies of energy to make our economy run — so I urge you to pass legislation to modernize our electricity system, promote conservation, and make America less dependent on foreign sources of energy.

My administration is promoting free and fair trade to open up new markets for America's entrepreneurs and manufacturers and farmers — to create jobs for American workers. Younger workers should have the opportunity to build a nest egg by saving part of their Social Security taxes in a personal retirement account. We should make the Social Security system a source of ownership for the American people. And we should limit the burden of government on this economy by acting as good stewards of taxpayers' dollars.

In two weeks, I will send you a budget that funds the war, protects the homeland, and meets important domestic needs, while limiting the growth in discretionary spending to less than 4 percent. This will require that Congress focus on priorities, cut wasteful spending, and be wise with the people's money. By doing so, we can cut the deficit in half over the next five years.

Tonight, I also ask you to reform our immigration laws so they reflect our values and benefit our economy. I propose a new temporary worker program to match willing foreign workers with willing employers when no Americans can be found to fill the job. This reform will be good for our economy because employers will find needed workers in an honest and orderly system. A temporary worker program will help protect our homeland, allowing Border Patrol and law enforcement to focus on true threats to our national security.

I oppose amnesty, because it would encourage further illegal immigration, and unfairly reward those who break our laws. My temporary worker program will preserve the citizenship path for those who respect the law, while bringing millions of hardworking men and women out from the shadows of American life.

Our nation's health care system, like our economy, is also in a time of change. Amazing medical technologies are improving and saving lives. This dramatic progress has brought its own challenge, in the rising costs of medical care and health insurance. Members of Congress, we must work together to help control those costs and extend the benefits of modern medicine throughout our country.

Meeting these goals requires bipartisan effort, and two months ago, you showed the way. By strengthening Medicare and adding a prescription drug benefit, you kept a basic commitment to our seniors: You are giving them the modern medicine they deserve.

Starting this year, under the law you passed, seniors can choose to receive a drug discount card, saving them 10 to 25 percent off the retail price of most prescription drugs — and millions of low-income seniors can get an additional $600 to buy medicine. Beginning next year, seniors will have new coverage for preventive screenings against diabetes and heart disease, and seniors just entering Medicare can receive wellness exams.

In January of 2006, seniors can get prescription drug

coverage under Medicare. For a monthly premium of about $35, most seniors who do not have that coverage today can expect to see their drug bills cut roughly in half. Under this reform, senior citizens will be able to keep their Medicare just as it is, or they can choose a Medicare plan that fits them best — just as you, as members of Congress, can choose an insurance plan that meets your needs. And starting this year, millions of Americans will be able to save money tax-free for their medical expenses in a health savings account.

I signed this measure proudly, and any attempt to limit the choices of our seniors, or to take away their prescription drug coverage under Medicare, will meet my veto.

On the critical issue of health care, our goal is to ensure that Americans can choose and afford private health care coverage that best fits their individual needs. To make insurance more affordable, Congress must act to address rapidly rising health care costs. Small businesses should be able to band together and negotiate for lower insurance rates, so they can cover more workers with health insurance. I urge you to pass association health plans. I ask you to give lower-income Americans a refundable tax credit that would allow millions to buy their own basic health insurance.

By computerizing health records, we can avoid dangerous medical mistakes, reduce costs, and improve care. To protect the doctor-patient relationship, and keep good doctors doing good work, we must eliminate wasteful and frivolous medical lawsuits. And tonight I propose that individuals who buy catastrophic health care coverage, as part of our new health savings accounts, be allowed to deduct 100 percent of the premiums from their taxes.

A government-run health care system is the wrong prescription. By keeping costs under control, expanding access, and helping more Americans afford coverage, we will preserve the system of private medicine that makes America's health care the best in the world.

We are living in a time of great change — in our world, in our economy, in science and medicine. Yet some things endure — courage and compassion, reverence and integrity, respect for differences of faith and race. The values we try to live by never change. And they are instilled in us by fundamental institutions, such as families and schools and religious congregations. These institutions, these unseen pillars of civilization, must remain strong in America, and we will defend them. We must stand with our families to help them raise healthy, responsible children. When it comes to helping children make right choices, there is work for all of us to do.

One of the worst decisions our children can make is to gamble their lives and futures on drugs. Our government is helping parents confront this problem with aggressive education, treatment, and law enforcement. Drug use in high school has declined by 11 percent over the last two years. Four hundred thousand fewer young people are using illegal drugs than in the year 2001. In my budget, I proposed new funding to continue our aggressive, community-based strategy to reduce demand for illegal drugs. Drug testing in our schools has proven to be an effective part of this effort. So tonight I proposed an additional $23 million for schools that want to use drug testing as a tool to save children's lives. The aim here is not to punish children, but to send them this message: We love you, and we don't want to lose you.

To help children make right choices, they need good examples. Athletics play such an important role in our society, but, unfortunately, some in professional sports are not setting much of an example. The use of performance-enhancing drugs like steroids in baseball, football, and other sports is dangerous, and it sends the wrong message — that there are shortcuts to accomplishment, and that performance is more important than character. So tonight I call on team owners, union representatives, coaches, and players to take the lead, to send the right signal, to get tough, and to get rid of steroids now.

To encourage right choices, we must be willing to confront the dangers young people face — even when they're difficult to talk about. Each year, about 3 million teenagers contract sexually-transmitted diseases that can harm them, or kill them, or prevent them from ever becoming parents. In my budget, I propose a grassroots campaign to help inform families about these medical risks. We will double federal funding for abstinence programs, so schools can teach this fact of life: Abstinence for young people is the only certain way to avoid sexually-transmitted diseases.

Decisions children now make can affect their health and character for the rest of their lives. All of us — parents and schools and government — must work together to counter the negative influence of the culture, and to send the right messages to our children.

A strong America must also value the institution of marriage. I believe we should respect individuals as we take a principled stand for one of the most fundamental, enduring institutions of our civilization. Congress has already taken a stand on this issue by passing the Defense of Marriage Act, signed in 1996 by President Clinton. That statute protects marriage under federal law as a union of a man and a woman, and declares that one state may not redefine marriage for other states.

Activist judges, however, have begun redefining marriage by court order, without regard for the will of the people and their elected representatives. On an issue of such great consequence, the people's voice must be heard. If judges insist on forcing their arbitrary will upon the people, the only alternative left to the people would be the constitutional process. Our nation must defend the sanctity of marriage.

The outcome of this debate is important — and so is the way we conduct it. The same moral tradition that defines marriage also teaches that each individual has dignity and value in God's sight.

It's also important to strengthen our communities by unleashing the compassion of America's religious institutions. Religious charities of every creed are doing some of the most vital work in our country — mentoring children, feeding the hungry, taking the hand of the lonely. Yet government has often denied social service grants and contracts to these groups, just because they have a cross or a Star of David or a crescent on the wall. By executive order, I have opened billions of dollars in grant money to competition that includes faith-based charities. Tonight I ask you to codify this into law, so people of faith can know that the law will never discriminate against them again.

In the past, we've worked together to bring mentors to children of prisoners, and provide treatment for the addicted, and help for the homeless. Tonight I ask you to consider another group of Americans in need of help. This year, some 600,000 inmates will be released from prison back into society. We know from long experience that if they can't find work, or a home, or help, they are much more likely to commit crime and return to prison. So tonight, I propose a four-year, $300 million prisoner re-entry initiative to expand job training and placement services, to provide transitional housing, and to help newly released prisoners get mentoring, including from faith-based groups. America is the land of second chance, and when the gates of the prison open, the path ahead should lead to a better life.

For all Americans, the last three years have brought tests we did not ask for, and achievements shared by all. By our actions, we have shown what kind of nation we are. In grief, we have found the grace to go on. In challenge, we rediscovered the courage and daring of a free people. In victory, we have shown the noble aims and good heart of America. And having come this far, we sense that we live in a time set apart.

I've been witness to the character of the people of

America, who have shown calm in times of danger, compassion for one another, and toughness for the long haul. All of us have been partners in a great enterprise. And even some of the youngest understand that we are living in historic times. Last month a girl in Lincoln, Rhode Island, sent me a letter. It began, "Dear George W. Bush. If there's anything you know, I, Ashley Pearson, age 10, can do to help anyone, please send me a letter and tell me what I can do to save our country." She added this P.S.: "If you can send a letter to the troops, please put, 'Ashley Pearson believes in you.'"

Tonight, Ashley, your message to our troops has just been conveyed. And, yes, you have some duties yourself. Study hard in school, listen to your mom or dad, help someone in need, and when you and your friends see a man or woman in uniform, say, "thank you." And, Ashley, while you do your part, all of us here in this great chamber will do our best to keep you and the rest of America safe and free.

My fellow citizens, we now move forward, with confidence and faith. Our nation is strong and steadfast. The cause we serve is right, because it is the cause of all mankind. The momentum of freedom in our world is unmistakable — and it is not carried forward by our power alone. We can trust in that greater power who guides the unfolding of the years. And in all that is to come, we can know that His purposes are just and true.

May God continue to bless America.

WOULD YOU LIKE MORE COPIES OF
GEORGE W. BUSH
SPEAKS TO THE NATION?

JUST MAIL IN OUR SIMPLE-TO-USE FORM HERE TO ORDER MORE COPIES!

-OR-

CALL (425) 454-7009!

DISCOUNT SCHEDULE

1 COPY	$9.95	25 COPIES	$174.14
5 COPIES	$39.80	50 COPIES	$248.75
10 COPIES	$79.60	100 COPIES	$497.50

Merril Press
P.O. Box 1682
Bellevue, WA 98009

Please send me_____copies of Wings of the Panther. Enclosed is my check or money order in the amount of $_____.

Please charge my: ☐Visa ☐Mastercard ☐AMEX ☐Discover

Number: _____Expires: _____

Signature:_____

Print Name: _____

Street: _____

City: _____ State: _____ Zip:_____

Phone: (_____)_____

Would you like more copies of
George W. Bush
Speaks to the Nation?

JUST MAIL IN OUR SIMPLE-TO-USE FORM HERE TO
ORDER MORE COPIES!

-OR-

Call (425) 454-7009!

DISCOUNT SCHEDULE

1 COPY	$9.95	25 COPIES	$174.14
5 COPIES	$39.80	50 COPIES	$248.75
10 COPIES	$79.60	100 COPIES	$497.50

Merril Press
P.O. Box 1682
Bellevue, WA 98009

Please send me_____copies of Wings of the Panther.
Enclosed is my check or money order in the amount
of $_____.

Please charge my: ☐Visa ☐Mastercard ☐AMEX ☐Discover

Number: _____Expires: _____

Signature:_____

Print Name: _____

Street: _____

City: _____ State: _____ Zip:_____

Phone: (_____)_____